John William Colenso, H. (Henricus) Oort

The Worship of Baalim in Israel

Based upon the Work of Dr. R. Dozy,

John William Colenso, H. (Henricus) Oort

The Worship of Baalim in Israel
Based upon the Work of Dr. R. Dozy,

ISBN/EAN: 9783744719629

Printed in Europe, USA, Canada, Australia, Japan

Cover: Foto ©ninafisch / pixelio.de

More available books at **www.hansebooks.com**

THE
WORSHIP OF BAALIM
IN ISRAEL.

BASED UPON THE WORK OF DR. R. DOZY,

'THE ISRAELITES AT MECCA.'

BY

DR. H. OORT

PASTOR OF SANTPOORT.

TRANSLATED FROM THE DUTCH,

AND ENLARGED WITH NOTES AND APPENDICES,

BY THE RIGHT REV.

JOHN WILLIAM COLENSO, D.D.

BISHOP OF NATAL.

LONDON:
LONGMANS, GREEN, AND CO.
1865.

PREFACE.

THE TREATISE, which is here laid before the English reader, is one of several, by different authors, that have been occasioned by the publication of the remarkable researches of Professor DOZY of Leyden, into the history of the ancient Sanctuary and Worship at Mecca, which he has traced—it would seem, very distinctly—to an Israelitish origin.

By continental critics, generally, Prof. Dozy's work has been cordially welcomed, not only as a specimen of most able, ingenious, and very original criticism, but as adding also considerably to our knowledge of the ancient affairs of Arabia, and throwing light upon some obscure points in the early history of Israel. It is natural, however, that, with respect to some of the details of so wide and difficult a subject, there should be room for difference of opinion, and, at all events, for a yet more close and searching examination. Accordingly, some of these details have been submitted to a separate investigation by more than one distinguished labourer in the field of Modern Biblical Criticism. And, indeed, it is only in this way, by the comparison of results arrived at by different processes of independent enquiry, and often from different points of view, that we may hope at length to arrive at definite conclusions, which may be ranked among the certainties of Science.

In the First Appendix to the Fifth Part of my Work on the Pentateuch I have given some account of Professor Dozy's researches: and, while engaged in passing that Part through the press, I have had before me several of these Treatises, especially those of OORT, *On the Worship of Baalim in Israel*, and *On*

Human Sacrifice in Israel, PIERSON, *On the Holy Stones in Israel,* and KUENEN, *On Baal-Worship in Israel,*—all written in Dutch, a language with which English scholars are not generally familiar, though some of the most valuable critical works of the present day, on the Old and New Testaments, are only to be read in Dutch originals. In the course of my own remarks, I have referred occasionally to the above-named writings. But I have felt that I should best serve the interests of Truth, in respect of the cause which I have at heart, and best satisfy the needs and, I trust, also the desires of English students, if I translated one or more of them, with additional notes, either confirming from my own point of view the positions of the writer, or else, where necessary, stating my reasons for dissenting from any of his conclusions.

With this view I have for the present selected for translation the very able Treatise of Dr. OORT. It will be seen that he touches all along on questions of great interest in relation to the main points of my own argument, as maintained in my Work on the Pentateuch, and especially in my Fifth Part, just published,—that he starts from premises somewhat different from mine, and arrives at somewhat different conclusions. Yet there is substantial agreement between us; and the differences of opinion, which I have expressed in the notes, are meant rather to *qualify,* than to *contradict,* his views, and tend, as it seems to me, to relieve them of some difficulties, and bring them more into agreement with those of Prof. DOZY. At any rate, I shall be satisfied to have thus placed more fully before English scholars for discussion the important questions which Professor DOZY and Dr. OORT have raised.

J. W. NATAL.

LONDON: *Aug.* 15, 1865.

THE
WORSHIP OF BAALIM
IN ISRAEL.

B

CONTENTS.

SECT.		PAGE
INTRODUCTION	. . . . . .	1—8
I. JHVH THE GOD OF ISRAEL	. . . .	9—34
II. MEANING OF THE BAAL AND THE BAALIM	. .	35—63
III. THE RELIGION OF THE EXPATRIATED SIMEONITES . .		64—78

APP.
I. ANALYSIS OF E.xx.1-17 . . .	. .	79
II. THE DEUTERONOMISTIC ORIGIN OF N.x.33-36	. .	80
III. THE LATER ORIGIN OF THE SONG OF DEBORAH .	.	81, 82
IV. THE COMPOSITE CHARACTER OF THE STORY OF GIDEON .	.	83—85
V. THE COMPOSITION OF HEBREW NAMES WITH THE DIVINE NAME	.	86—94

N.B. By *P.I*,*P.II*,&c., reference is made to the First, Second &c. Parts of my Work on the Pentateuch.

INTRODUCTION.

1. A FEW months ago appeared the work of Dr. R. DOZY, Professor at Leyden, entitled *The Israelites at Mecca, from the time of David to the fifth century of our Era.* The object of it is to show that the ancient Sanctuary of Mecca was founded about David's reign,[1] by a body of emigrating, or rather expatriated,[2] Israelites of the tribe of Simeon,—that these established the great Festival of Mecca, the origin and meaning of which has hitherto lain in obscurity,—and, lastly, that in the time of the Babylonish Captivity a second colony of Israelites, called by the Arabians 'the Second Gorhum,'[3] arrived at Mecca.

2. The consequences, that follow from these conjectures,— which are supported by so many proofs of various kinds that

---

[1] This statement of Dr. OORT, 'about David's reign,' agrees more closely with my own view (*P.V.App.*I.11-14) than with that of Dr. DOZY, who supposes that the movement in question may have taken place in *the latter part of Saul's reign*, *p.*56,59. But the difference in time is, of course, very inconsiderable; and, indeed, Dozy himself speaks elsewhere, *p.*17, of its having happened in 'the time of David,' and on *p.*94 he leaves the matter doubtful:—'Whether they thus settled themselves at Mecca at the time of Saul's reign, or perhaps at the time of David's, I must leave undecided; and, if any one chooses to read in my Title 'Saul' instead of 'David,' I can as little show that he is wrong, as he on the other hand can show that he is right.' But see the reasons given by me for 'the reign of David' in *P.V.App.*I.12,14.

[2] According to my view (*P.V.App.*I.18) this movement of the Simeonites was a regular *migration*,—'chiefly for want of room, and to relieve the necessities of their condition as described in G.xlix.7,'—and was not occasioned by a sentence of exile, for their remissness in the war with Amalek, as Prof. Dozy supposes.

[3] According to Dozy, 'Gorhum'=גרים, 'sojourners' or 'strangers'; for 'the change of *garim* or *gerim* into *gorhum* or *gurhum* has nothing strange in the mouth of an Arabian,' DOZY, *p.*105. The Simeonites, of course, were the 'First Gorhum.'

in my opinion they stand incontestably confirmed,—are of the highest importance. In the first place, Prof. Dozy's results are of inestimable value for those who are engaged in the study of Arabian History and Literature; since they supply the key to innumerable riddles, and throw light for them upon the darkest questions: and, building on upon the foundations here laid by Dozy, they may probably discover new facts of still greater interest.

3. But the respected Author does not desire only to furnish an important contribution for the knowledge of Arabian History; he wishes also to do this at the same time for the people of Israel; and he hopes that, from the new point of view here opened, a light may be thrown upon the original Israelitish worship. This expectation is very natural. If the dîn Ibrahîm, the old religion in Arabia, which it was Mohammed's object to restore, was a remainder of the religion of the Simeonites, who had founded the Sanctuary,—if the great Festival of Islam was originally an Israelitish Feast,—then we have here given us a new source of help towards the knowledge of the religious condition of Israel about the time when the tribe of Simeon emigrated.

4. Something of this kind was very greatly needed: for, as every one knows, the sources, from which we are obliged to derive the knowledge of that time, are scanty and not always even trustworthy. The writers and compilers of those Books, which communicate to us certain particulars about it, give us frequently all along, either in good faith or of set purpose, a distorted image of it. One after another, Prophets, Priests, and Rabbies, regarding the history of ancient times from their own point of view, have done their best to hide from us the truth. It is one-sided when Prof. Dozy lays the blame only on the men of the Great Synagogue: Prophets and Priests before them have done no less than they.

5. In the lapse of ages the religion of Israel was unspeak-

ably changed; so that, from what it was a few centuries after the Captivity, it is impossible to make out its condition five centuries before that event. Those, who give us the history of that time, believed that the orthodox worship of their own days was the original, and that every variation from it in former centuries, as well as in their own time, was to be called an apostasy. And under the influence of this conviction, they have frequently allowed themselves the liberty of colouring the facts in accordance with their own views.[4]

6. The Israelitish worship at Mecca has not had the same development. *There* were no Prophets, Priests, or Rabbies, who thought it necessary, in the interest of their own convictions, to set forth incorrectly the ancient state of things. Hence there is ground for hoping that at Mecca facts may be brought to light, in reference to the ancient religious worship of Israel, the traces of which may have wholly or nearly disappeared in the Books of the Old Testament.

7. But, in drawing conclusions from what existed at Mecca to what may have also existed in Canaan, we must not forget that the fate of this ancient tribe also has not remained unchanged, nor been handed down to us, traditionally, with certainty. It is probable, no doubt, that the religion of the Simeonites, cut loose from the Holy Land, may have come rapidly to a standstill, and that no such a fermentation may have taken place in it as in Judah: but it cannot all at once have turned into stone.

8. The amalgamation of the Simeonites with the Minæi (DOZY, *p.*74,75), from whom they had conquered their new fatherland, or with other surrounding Arabian tribes, must also have had an influence. The 'Second Gorhum,' the refugee settlers from Cutha, though they adapted themselves to the habits of their countrymen whom they found already living at Mecca,

---

[4] This remark is especially true of the history as told by the Chronicler: see P.V.271.

did not, we may be sure, submit themselves passively to everything. Lastly, the greater portion of this 'Gorhum' was driven from the holy soil of Mecca by the Chozaha; and these last were so far from leaving the old religion unchanged that, according to the Arabian tradition, they greatly corrupted it (Dozy,*p.*203).

9. Thus the religion of the Simeonites at Mecca existed for about fifteen centuries amidst constant vicissitudes,[5] before we have any account of it,—reason enough why we should not instantly draw conclusions from what existed in Mohammed's time to what the Simeonites brought with them. The book of Dozy itself shows clearly what changes took place at Mecca: see the accounts about '*maqâm Ibrahîm*,' '*Isâf* and *Nâïla*,' &c. We shall return to speak on some points presently.

10. In fact, the religion of the Israelites in Palestine and that of the Simeonites at Mecca are as two twin-sisters, who, parted in youth from one another, have experienced heaven-wide differences of education; so that in their old age they do not at all resemble each other, while they have, both of them, merely slight reminiscences of that which has made them what they are. Accurate study of character, however, may still be able—from traces of agreement, brought into connection with what they each remember of their former course of life—to make out what they were in the days of their youth. We *may*, therefore, and we *must*, make use of this new means of help, provided only that we do not forget that we possess here no *photograph* of the Simeonitish religion, but only a *blurred sketch* of it.

11. Dr. Dozy, however, has not contented himself with indicating the pre-Islamite religion of the Arabians as a help

[5] We are scarcely, perhaps, justified in saying '*constant* vicissitudes'; though Dr. OORT has enumerated, no doubt, *some* great causes of disturbance, which may have affected materially the worship at Mecca at different points of time in this long interval.

towards understanding the ancient Israelitish religion. He has also quoted some phenomena, which in his opinion characterised the religion of the Simeonites,—has inferred that these, consequently, belonged to the old Israelitish religion,—and has endeavoured to show that the reminiscence of these has remained in the Books of the Old Testament.

12. Has he in this reasoned correctly? He found himself on slippery ground. We are easily tempted, if we imagine that we have found a track which leads to surprising results, to follow that track, and, in so doing, while placing one-sidedly in the foreground whatever seems to prove its correctness, to close the eye to whatever may be urged to the contrary. Men easily find what they wish to find: many sharp-witted scholars are thus often led upon a false path.

13. While Dozy has been eminently successful in the explanation of some puzzling questions,—as, for instance, in his identification of the Meccan Festival with the solemnities observed anciently by the Israelites, probably at the Gilgal,— on other points, as it appears to me, he has entirely failed. With reference to one subject of the greatest interest I wish to show this,—I mean, with reference to his attempt to prove that the ancient religion of Israel was not a worship of JHVH, but of Baal, *because Baal was the Deity worshipped by the Simeonites*.[6]

[6] It will be seen that the view, which I have advanced in Part V, lies midway between those of Dr. Dozy and Dr. Oort, and would, if approved, serve as the meeting-point of both. It appears to me that the 'ancient religion of Israel,'— that is, their religion in the time of David,—was the worship of JHVH (IAO, Adonis, the Sun) as 'the Baal' of Canaan, the 'Lord' of the Syro-Phœnician tribes, from whom they adopted this worship after their occupation of the land.

Of course, this supposes that the Israelites did *not* arrive in Canaan, as the Scripture story says, in full panoply of war, with a grand national religion of their own, already highly developed, as in the Book of Deuteronomy, and a splendid ritual fully established. It assumes that they came out of Egypt, (as the Egyptian traditions seem to imply, which connect them with *leprosy*,) in a low and impoverished state, and found their way into Canaan rather as a straggling horde of separate tribes,—numerous, no doubt, and strong enough to struggle on, until they

14. This last fact (italicised), according to Dozy, appears from the following circumstances.

(i) The chief deity worshipped in the Temple at Mecca was called *Hobal*, *i.e.* *hab-Baal*, 'the Baal.'

(ii) Beside the image of the god, there was a *well* serving as a treasury: and since in Jo.xix.8, among the towns of the Simeonites, we find also 'Baal-of-the-Well' (בעל הבאר), it is probable that this Baal was the Baal proper of the Simeonites.

(iii) The place, which was afterwards called 'Mecca,' was named anciently 'Gedôr-Baal,' *i. e.* 'Baal's Enclosure' or 'Baal's Sanctuary.' This name is found nowhere in the O.T. uncorrupted. But the unintelligible 'Gur-Baal' of 2Ch.xxvi.7 must be changed into 'Gedôr-Baal,' [*i.c.* גור into גדר], and the same must be read

---

at last got a footing in the land, but for some time after their arrival (as the Bible itself tells us) harassed by a variety of conquerors and oppressors. In short, it assumes (what the Book of Judges clearly shows, when carefully studied) that, before the time of Samuel, Israel had no political or religious organisation whatever.

Coming thus, without any definite religion of their own (see 91)—or, perhaps, bringing with them only some remnant of the religious notions which prevailed in Egypt, Ez.xx.7,8, and which they would be ready enough to discard as 'hateful' (see 116)—and settling among the Canaanites (Phœnicians), who were possessed already of a high civilisation, (*comp.* the nine hundred iron chariots of Jabin, Ju.iv.3, however the story may be exaggerated,) and were possessed also of a fully developed religion,—it is most natural that they should have readily adopted the worship of JHVH, the 'God of the land.' Dr. OORT says (116), 'An oppressed people will never adopt the religion of its oppressors, unless it is absorbed in them, and loses its nationality.' With this I fully agree: but the Israelites in *Canaan* were not exactly the 'oppressed,' nor the Canaanites the 'oppressors.' In *Egypt* the former were, as the traditions clearly imply, altogether oppressed and down-trodden: in *Canaan* they appear at first rather as the *oppressors*; and, though at times down-trodden—sometimes by *Syrians*, Ju.iii.8, and *Canaanites*, Ju.iv.2, at other times by foreign foes, *Moabites*, iii.14, *Midianites*, vi.1, *Ammonites*, x.7, *Philistines*, xiii.1, from whose invasions, no doubt, the Canaanites also suffered,— yet they constantly recovered themselves again, and maintained themselves in possession of the greater part—and at last of the whole—of the land.

To the common people, no doubt, JHVH was always 'the Baal,' even down to the time of the Captivity, and was worshipped as such with impure rites and bloody sacrifices. But the great Prophets of Israel, under Divine Teaching,— beginning, most probably, with Samuel,—were always striving with this idolatry, and seeking to raise the people from these gross notions to the idea of JHVH, as the Living God. In future, it will be convenient to use 'JHVH' or 'IAO' in speaking expressly of the *heathen* view of the Deity, which was shared by the people of Israel, generally, and 'JEHOVAH,' when referring to the higher, more spiritual, view of His Character, as entertained by the Prophets.

also in 1Ch.iv.39, (where the place is named simply Gedôr,) by slightly modifying the following word, [*i.e.* changing נדר עד into נדר בעל].[7]

(iv) Baal is the planet Saturn; and Mahommedans of the twelfth century after Christ knew still that the Meccan Sanctuary was anciently dedicated to Saturn.

15. Meanwhile the O.T. tells us that JHVH, and not Baal, was the God of Israel. But this, according to Professor Dozy, is a *pia fraus* of the orthodox Jews of later centuries, to which the writers and compilers of these Books belonged. And it is still possible to discover some traces of the truth, such as the following:—

(i) Amos tells us, v.25,26, that the so-called 'Tabernacle,' the Mosaic Sanctuary, was dedicated to Saturn (Chiun or Cheivân), *i.e.* Baal, so that a Sanctuary of Baal stood at Shiloh, *p.*27, just as a Feast of Baal took place at the Gilgal, *p.*112, *comp. p.*142.

(ii) The same is shown by the fact that the place, where the Ark stood in Samuel's days, known afterwards as 'Kirjath-Jearim,' was formerly called 'Kirjath-Baal' (=Baal's-Town), or simply 'Baal,' 1Ch.xiii.6.

(iii) 'Israel' is one of the names given by the Phœnicians in later days to Saturn (SANCHON., *p.*42, *ed. Orell.*).

(iv) A worship of Baal or Saturn is also implied by the consecration of the 'seventh day' of the week and of the number 'seven' generally; and Jews of the fifteenth century named also the planet Saturn 'Sabbethai' and 'the Star of Israel.'

(v) The strongest proof, however, that the worship of Baal went hand in hand with that of JHVH, and existed as lawful worship till David's time, is the fact that the name Baal occurs in several Proper Names,—among others, in those of the sons of Saul and David, *viz.* Esh*baal*, Merib*baal*, *Baal*yadah. The Compiler of the Books of Samuel, or later Rabbies, who disliked this, changed these names into Ishbosheth, Mephibosheth, Elyadah: but in the parallel passages of the Chronicles the original names are still preserved.

16. The supposition that a Baal-worship existed lawfully in Israel superior, or even next,[8] to the worship of JHVH, is in

---

[7] See these points of Prof. Dozy's argument exhibited in full in my *P.V. App.*I.37-41.

[8] The view maintained by me, in *P.V.*Chap.XIX-XXI, is, that the worship of JEHOVAH developed itself gradually out of the worship of JHVH, 'the Baal' of Canaan,—that, consequently, the worship of 'the Baal' was neither above nor below the worship of JHVH, but in the oldest times—*i.e.* probably, until the age of Samuel—they were simply *identical*,—the name JHVH having been adopted by the Hebrews, after the conquest of Canaan, or else adapted by a slight modification (*i.e.* by the change of יחוה into יהוה) from the mysterious name of the Sun-God

my opinion incorrect. I shall show this first from the O.T., in order then to go on and investigate the connection which existed between the worship of the Baalim and of JHVH. We will, finally, fix our attention upon the Temple at Mecca, and enquire whether the phenomena, which present themselves there, are such as to negative our conclusion.

among the northern tribes of Syro-Phœnicia, the two names being represented in Greek, by profane and Christian writers, by the very same letters IAΩ.

Accordingly, we find Phœnician names compounded with *Jah*, just exactly as Hebrew names, *e.g.* 'Αβδαῖος = Obad*iah*, *Bithias* = Bith*iah*, *comp.* Abdi*el*, Bethu*el* (*P.*V.339). So Rezon, the Syrian of Zobah, was the son of *El*yadah, 1K.xi.23, in the very same age when David's son was called *Baal*yadah, 1Ch.xiv.7, who appears also as *El*yadah in 2S.v.16. This seems to show an identity of worship in *Syria* and *Israel*; *comp.* the similar conversion of *Baal*berith, Ju.ix.4, into *El*berith, Ju.ix.46. This identity, however, is exhibited still more distinctly in the fact that in 2.S.viii.10, the son of Toi, the Syrian King of Hamath, is actually called *Jo*ram, *i.e.*, *Jeho*ram, (= 'JHVH is exalted'), which name appears in 1Ch.xviii.10 as *Hado*ram. But *Hado*ram is also the name of an officer of Rehoboam in 2Ch.x.18, who appears as *Ado*ram in 1K.xii.18, and as *Ado*niram in 1K.iv.6, v.14. See *App.*V.

It will be found, as we proceed, that the above view gets rid of some difficulties, and explains some doubtful points, in the views both of OORT and DOZY, and, in fact, as has been said already (note *), may help, if approved by scholars, to reconcile them.

SECTION I.

JHVH THE GOD OF ISRAEL.

17. IF Baal was anciently the chief Deity of the Israelitish tribes, so that his worship was the lawful, official worship in the days of Moses, and long afterwards, whence, then, came the worship of JHVH?[9] Will it be maintained that this was first

> [9] This question has been answered from my own point of view in *P.V.* Chap.XIX-XXI: see the preceding note.
> I should not say with Prof. DOZY, as quoted by Dr. OORT, that 'Baal was the *chief* Deity of the Israelitish tribes': rather the Sun was '*the* Baal,' '*the* Lord,' the *only* Deity worshipped by the *people*, generally, in the days of Saul and David. Nor, taking into account the unhistorical character of the story of the Exodus in the Pentateuch, and especially that of the conquest of Canaan by Joshua,—since half the Book of Joshua is Deuteronomistic (*P.V.*5), and the rest of it, probably, not older than the time of David or Solomon (*P.V.*212)—can I see ground for assuming, as a matter of fact, that there was *any* 'lawful, official worship' established 'in the days of Moses' or for some time after the Exodus. My view is, rather, that the Israelites entered Canaan, probably in large numbers, but as a mere undisciplined horde, and settled down among the inhabitants of the district as they best could, fighting here, intriguing there, but practically, in no long time, overrunning the land. They must probably have had some leader, such as Moses, on their march out of Egypt: but the Bible itself tells us that he died before they entered Canaan. And, as to Joshua, he appears to be entirely a mythical character, most of his great exploits having been recorded only by the Deuteronomist in Josiah's time, and apparently from his own imagination, not even from legendary traditions about him, if any could be supposed to have been handed down vividly through the lapse of eight centuries. For, surely, if such legends were current in the days of Josiah,—and retained so strongly in the recollections of the people, that the Deuteronomist could undertake the task of collecting them, and recording them permanently on parchment,—*we should find some trace* of the renown of this great Conqueror in the Psalms and Prophets: whereas his very name is never once mentioned.
> In short, my view is that there was no 'lawful official worship' in Israel, till

entirely overshadowed by Baal-worship, then existed in combination with it, and at last expelled it?[10] This is, in truth, a very improbable supposition. That among a people, which worships many gods, it should happen through various circumstances that now one, now another, should be more highly honoured, is very natural—but not that a people should change its national religion for another, unless it loses also its national character, and thus becomes, as it were, another nation.[11]

the time of David, when the Tabernacle was erected on Mount Zion. In the Tabernacle at Shiloh, apparently the *chief* Sanctuary in the days of the Judges, 'the Baal' of Syria was worshipped; and possibly as early as Eli's time, or even earlier, the Name JHVH was used in Israel, but not with the high spiritual meaning which was attached to that Name in later days: for the account in 1S.i–iii is manifestly a composition out of a much later age—perhaps that of Solomon (*P.V.App*.III.23, see note **),—and reflects the spirit and views of the writer, living two centuries after the birth of Samuel. This 'worship of JHVH,' then, 'came from' the Canaanites; especially, the Name 'JHVH' seems to have been derived from the more advanced worship of the Syro-Phœnician tribes in the north of Palestine. But 'the Baal,' the Sun-God, was 'the God of the land' throughout the whole district: and, if his chief place of worship for Israel was at Shiloh, yet 'the Baalim,' as representatives of 'the Baal,' were doubtless worshipped in various places, as is indicated by the names *Baal-Berith, Baal-Gad, Baal-Hamon, Baal-Hazor, Baal-Hermon, Baal-Meon, Baal-Perazim, Baal-Zephon, Baal-Shalisha, Baal-Beer, Baal-Tamar*, &c.: comp. also *Beth-Shemesh*, 'House of the Sun,' with *Beth-El*, 'House of El,' and note *En-Shemesh*, 'Fountain of the Sun,' Jo.xv.7,xviii.17, *Ir-Shemesh*, 'City of the Sun,' Jo.xix.41, *Kheres*, 'the Sun,' Ju.i.35, *Timnath-Kheres*, 'Timnah of the Sun,' Ju.ii.9. Comp. also the mythic Hebrew Hercules, Samson (שִׁמְשׁוֹן, 'the Sun'). If even these names were all given originally by the ancient Canaanites, they would prove (i) that 'the Baal' was the *Sun*, and (ii) that Sun-worship was at that time common in the land; and the whole history teaches us that the Israelites made such names their own, by adopting the worship of 'the Baalim' all over the land, as in the case of Gideon's father, who had 'an altar of the Baal,' Ju.vi.25.

[10] No! Before Samuel's time JHVH-worship *was* Baal-worship, and such it continued to be for the mass of the people, even down to the time of the Captivity. Only in every age, from Samuel downwards, a few of higher mind were Divinely taught to look themselves, and strove—but for the most part in vain—to teach their people to look, above JHVH, the Sun-God, to JEHOVAH, the living Elohim, who made 'the Sun to rule by day, and the Moon by night.'

[11] It will be seen that our view does not require this 'unnatural' supposition. We do not imagine that the Hebrews, on coming out of Egypt, where (if the tradition is to be relied on at all) they had been living in an abject and miserable condition, had any particular national Deity. They most probably worshipped the gods of Egypt (see Ez.xx.7,8), and followed to some extent the Egyptian customs.

18. Every people of antiquity, every tribal confederation, had its God, after whom it was named, in whose name it was summoned to battle, by whom solemn oaths were taken. This God protected his people and fought for it; so that, from the more or fewer victories which the people gained, the might or weakness of its God appeared, 2K.xix.12. And, naturally, each people regarded its own God as the God of Gods. Moab was the people of Chemosh, N.xxi.29, Jer.xlviii.7,13, 1K.xi.7,33, 2K.xxiii.13; Ammon's God was Milchom, 2K.xxiii.13, anciently,—perhaps when that people was more closely united with the Moabites, —also Chemosh, Ju.xi.24; that of the Philistines was Dagon, Ju.xvi.23, 1S.v.2, that of the Sidonians, Astarte, 1K.xi.5,33.[12]

19. 'No people ever fell away from its God.' This was in Jeremiah's days a well-known truism, which led him to exclaim to Israel, ii.11:—

'Has ever a nation changed its God, though it is no God? Yet my people has changed its Glory for a thing of naught.'

But they had no attachment to this worship as a national worship inherited from their fathers, and would very naturally—if only to ingratiate themselves with the people of the land—adopt the worship which they found in Canaan. And this is just exactly what they did, according to the statements of the Bible itself, though in later Deuteronomistic notices, Ju.ii.11-13, &c. But even the Elohistic story implies that they knew nothing about JHVH till the time of the Exodus, E.vi.2-7, which seems to be based on the historical fact, that they knew nothing of it before they left Egypt and (probably after a short—not forty years'—wandering) entered into Canaan.

Nor again, is there any sign, as it seems to me, of any definite 'national character' having been formed among them, till the time of Samuel's efforts for the organisation of the whole community, the progress of which was somewhat interrupted during the reign of Saul, but brought to completion under David.

The adoption of the religion of Canaan by the invading Israelites may perhaps be paralleled with the adoption of Christianity by the northern barbarians, who made their irruptions into the Roman Empire.

[12] But, even according to the Pentateuch itself, JHVH was *not* the God of Israel *before* the time of Moses, E.vi.2-7: and this account of the Elohist of Samuel's time seems to point, as we have argued, to the historical fact, that JHVH was not really known to the Israelites until they left Egypt and settled in Canaan; while other indications seem to show, as I have argued in Part V, that in Samuel's days JHVH had been only recently set forth—probably, by Samuel himself—as JEHOVAH, the Living God, the God of Israel.

It may be said, in answer to this complaint, that the Israel of Jeremiah's days was, according to the Prophet himself, an example of a people changing its God. But be it remembered that here an ambassador is speaking, who characterised, as revolt from JHVH, whatever in the popular religion was in his view unlawful, whatever practice conflicted with his own idea of JHVH-ism. Although in Jeremiah's time the Gods of Judah were even 'more in number than their cities,' Israel was still, nevertheless, then as ever, the people of JHVH.

20. The language of the Prophets, who continually reproached the people with forsaking JHVH,—the notices of the writers of Judges and Samuel, who knew no other causes of national affliction than idolatry, and constantly ascribed the miseries of Israel to that source,—might easily lead us on a false track. Before the Captivity, Israel was absolutely not in the possession of Monotheism. A few might raise themselves to this height; but the mass of the people were thorough-going polytheists. Still, that did not prevent JHVH remaining all along the God of Israel.[13] An anti-JHVH-istic worship was never popular in Israel.

21. How deeply, indeed, the reverence for JHVH had penetrated the heart, not merely of Priests and Prophets, but of the People, appears from the religious history of the northern kingdom. Surely, if in the days of Saul and David JHVH stood in the shadow of Baal,—nay, had even his place contested, as the God of Israel,—then it is inexplicable that Jeroboam, the son of Nebat, should have established a worship of JHVH, of which fact, however, there can be no doubt.[14] He would rather, in

---

[13] Certainly, JHVH remained all along the God of Israel,—that is, as we suppose, from the time when Samuel and the prophets of his school first introduced the idea of JEHOVAH being the Covenant-God of Israel.

[14] It is not at all inexplicable if, in the eyes of the people, JHVH was the same as the Baal. And that this was the case we gather from the fact that both Saul and David had sons whose names were compounded with Baal, viz. Esh*baal*, *Baal*yadah (15.v), as well as others whose names were compounded with JHVH, as *Jo*nathan, 1S.xiii.2, Adoni*jah*, Shephat*iah*, 2S.iii.4. Accordingly, at Byblus, Adonis (JHVH)

opposition to Solomon's temple-worship, have done homage to Baal.[15] Under Ahab, the worship of the Tyrian Baal was introduced—or at least favoured—by the king.[16] Violent was

had a famous temple in common with the goddess *Baaltis*, Von der ALM, I.*p*.494, 495. And, that the worship established by Jeroboam was really the worship of JHVH, the Baal of the tribes of Canaan, is plain from his setting up *calves*,— or, rather, *heifers*, see notes [17, 11a]—as symbols of the Deity, 1K.xii.28-30. Von der ALM observes, I.*p*.477:—'The steer was in all West-Asiatic religions, and also with the Egyptians, the image of the Sun-God. Doubtless, the usefulness and strength of this animal determined its being chosen as the symbol of this Deity.' Accordingly, by the calf at Bethel was set up an Ashera, 2K.xxiii.15, just as in the Temple of JHVH at Jerusalem, 2K.xxiii.6,—that is, a *phallus*, note [a], the symbol of the worship of Adonis, which is so constantly connected with 'the Baal,' E.xxxiv.13, D.v.ii.5, xii.3, 1K.xiv.23, 2K.xvii.10, xxiii.14, Mic.v.12,13, and *comp*. 2K.xvii.16—'And they made them molten images, even two *calves*, and made an *Ashera*, and worshipped all the host of heaven, and *served the Baal*.'

And, if the mention of 'the host of heaven' leaves a doubt whether the expression 'served the Baal' may not be used here in a more general sense, for idolatrous worship of any kind, yet we read more distinctly in Tob.i.4,5,—'All the tribe of Nephtali my father fell from the House of Jerusalem, which was chosen out of all the tribes of Israel, that all the tribes should sacrifice there, where the Temple of the Habitation of the Most High was consecrated and built for all ages. Now all the tribes which revolted together, and the house of my father Nephthali, sacrificed *to the Baal the heifer*.' See especially note [17].

[18] Jeroboam's object was not to prevent the people recognising JHVH as the God of Israel, but to prevent their *going up to Jerusalem*, 1K.xii.27. And, in fact, the worship of JHVH was, probably, not more corrupt under Jeroboam at Dan and Bethel, than it was in Judah under his rival Rehoboam, under whose reign we read, 1K.xiv.22-24,—

'Judah did evil in the sight of JEHOVAH, and they provoked Him to jealousy with their sins which they had committed, above all that their fathers had done. And they also built them high-places, and statues, and asheras, upon every high hill and under every green tree. And there was also the sodomite (lit. 'holy-one,' *i.e.* consecrated to the Deity) in the land: they did according to all the abominations of the nations which Jehovah drave-out before the sons of Israel.'

[16] Ahab, at the instance of his wife Jezebel, introduced the worship of the *Tyrian* Baal,—called by the Greeks 'the Tyrian Heracles'—still the Sun-God, but worshipped under a different name [a] and, probably, with different rites—especially,

---

[a] Some, as MUNTER, *Rel. der Karth. p.*41, and HAMAKER, *Misc. Phœn. p*.240, derive this name 'Herakles' from הָרְכָל, *harachal*, 'he who goes about,' *comp*. Ps.xix.6. But MOVERS, i.*p*.430-2, rejects this derivation, and, appealing to the name 'Ἀρχαλεύς, the son of Phœnix, the founder of Gades, *Etym. Mag*., he derives it from אַרכל, *Archal*, of which word the first half, meaning 'Fire,' occurs in the word *Ariel*, Is.xxix.1,2,7, and the last half is found in Jehu*chal* or Ju*chal*, Jer. xxxvii.3,xxxviii.1, = 'Jah prevails,' *comp*. G.xxxii.25.28, Hos.xii.3,4.—ED.

the opposition, sharp the conflict, and quickly was it decided: and Jehu put an end to this worship for ever.[17]

with a dreadful system of human sacrifices (*P.V.p.*293). So JOSEPHUS says, *Ant.* VIII.xiii.1—'Ahab married the daughter of Ithobal (Ethbaal), the King of the Tyrians and Sidonians, whose name was Jezebel, from whom he learned to worship her Gods. For this woman was energetic and daring, and went on to such a pitch of shameless madness, that she even built a temple to the Tyrian Deity, whom they call Bel.' And again he says, *Ant.*IX.vi.5,—'This Baal was the God of the Tyrians. And Ahab, wishing to gratify his stepfather Ithobal, King of the Tyrians and Sidonians, built a temple to him.' But JHVH was the *Syrian* Baal, the God of Byblus and Lebanon (*P.V.App.*III.11, Mov.i.*p.*176,181,188,195), though (as we have said) the Sun-God still, in all cases. Mov.i. *p.*184.

As the *Tyrian* Baal was, apparently, not known in Israel till the time of Ahab, it is plain that 'the Baal,' to whom Gideon's surname 'Jerubbaal' refers, must have been the *Syrian* or *Syro-Phœnician* Baal, Adonis-IAO. Perhaps, the worship of this *Syrian* Baal was more easy, sensual, and lascivious, than the severer and stricter worship of the *Tyrian* Baal.

[17] Jehu rooted-out the worship of the *Tyrian* Baal, introduced by Jezebel, but not that of the *Syrian* Baal; for we are expressly told that, though Jehu 'destroyed the Baal out of Israel,' yet he 'departed not from the sins of Jeroboam the son of Nebat, who made Israel to sin, the golden calves of Bethel and Dan.' 2K.x.28,29. And, accordingly, we find the worship of the calves of Bethaven (=Bethel) referred to in the days of Jehu's great-grandson, Jeroboam, by the prophet Hosea, viii.5,6, x.5, whereas in ii.8,17, the people of Samaria are spoken of as still serving 'the Baal' or 'the Baalim': and both in ii.8 and xiii.1 the LXX has τῇ Βάαλ, where the feminine article is explained by the more full expression in Tob.i.5, ἔθυον τῇ Βάαλ τῇ δαμάλει, 'they sacrificed to the Baal the heifer'; *comp.* 2K.x.29, αἱ δαμάλεις αἱ χρυσαῖ ἐν Βαιθηλ καὶ ἐν Δάν, 'the golden heifers in Bethel and in Dan,' and see also the LXX version of 1K.xii.28–32, where δάμαλις, 'heifer,' is continually used.

And so writes Von der ALM, i.*p.*511:—'Jehu, it is true, at the instance of the prophets, extirpated the worship of [the Tyrian] Baal: but it is not recorded that he burnt also the *Asheras.* Rather, we find from 2K.xiii.6 that Jehu's son and follower, Jehoahaz, like his father, maintained the worship of the calf [ἡ Βάαλ ἡ δάμαλις] at Bethel, and, it is added, the Ashera remained standing in Samaria.' This was, no doubt, the famous Ashera which Ahab made, 1K.xvi.33, and which Manasseh seems to have copied, 2K.xxi.3, and which was at last burnt by Josiah, 2K.xxiii.15. It was, probably, not connected particularly with the worship of the Tyrian Baal, which Jehu extirpated, but belonged to the old worship of JHVH, which he did not wish to abolish. We read, indeed, of '450 prophets of the Baal and 400 prophets of the Ashera, who ate at Jezebel's table,' 1K.xviii.19; so that this Tyrian Princess patronised *both* forms of worship; and, in fact, the name of her daughter, 'Athal*iah*,' 2K.viii.18,26, was compounded with JHVH. And these were all assembled by Elijah on Mount Carmel. But it is noticeable that *only* 'the 450 prophets of the Baal' are addressed by the prophet, and said to have been

22. Especially, let it be observed that, when the northern kingdom had been carried captive, and so the best part of the people was no longer in the land, but had made way for

killed by his orders, 1K.xviii.22,25,40: so that even Elijah is not represented as judging so severely 'the prophets of the Ashera,' that is, apparently, the prophets of the *old* worship of the *Syrian* Baal.

Also, these same '400 prophets,' apparently, are called together by Ahab, as prophets of JHVH, and they reply in the name of JHVH, 1K.xxii.5,6, and so Micaiah is spoken of as 'a prophet of JHVH *besides*,' v.7,8. It seems plain, therefore, that the prophets of the Ashera at Bethel,—who were, of course, prophets of 'the Baal the heifer' there,—were regarded as 'prophets of JHVH,'—in other words, that 'the Baal' of Bethel was identified by the people with JHVH.

Further, it is evident from Hos.iv.15—' Though thou, Israel, play the harlot, yet let not Judah offend; and come ye not to the Gilgal, neither go ye up to Bethaven (Bethel), and swear ye not, Life of JHVH! (JHVH for ever!)'—that the people of *Judah* were in the habit of frequenting these high-places of Israel at the Gilgal and at Bethel. But so also the people of Israel seem to have been in the habit of attending some similar idolatrous worship at *Beersheba*, in the south of Judah, Am.v.5—' Seek ye not Bethel, neither come ye to the Gilgal, and pass not to Beersheba,'—and again, viii.14, 'They that swear by the transgression of Samaria (=the heifer at Bethel,) and say 'Thy God for ever, O Dan!' and 'The way of Beersheba for ever!'.' It would seem that at each of these places, Bethel, Dan, the Gilgal, Beersheba, there were well-known festivals connected with the worship of JHVH, 'the Baal' of Canaan, the 'God of the land,'—and that the symbol of the Deity at Dan and Bethel,—if not also at Gilgal and Beersheba, and perhaps other places in both kingdoms—was a *heifer* (δάμαλις), which accounts, perhaps, for the LXX using often the feminine article, which some refer to εἰκών, 'image,' understood.

It may be useful to collect here in one view the different forms of expression employed by the LXX for 'the Baal' and 'the Baalim':—

ὁ Βάαλ, Ju.ii.13, vi.25,28,30,31,32, viii.33, 1K.xvi.31,32, xviii.22,26,40, xix.18, 2K.iii.2, x.18,19,20,21,22,23,25,26,27,28, xi.18, xvii.16, xxiii.4,5;

ἡ Βάαλ, 2K.xxi.3, Jer.ii.8,23,28, vii.9, xi.13,17, xii.16, xix.5, xxiii.13,27, Hos.ii.8, xiii.1, Zeph.i.4;

N.B. Jeremiah has *always* ἡ Βάαλ; in Rom.xi.4 ἡ Βάαλ stands for ὁ Βάαλ of 1K.xix.18;

Βάαλ, 1K.xviii.21, 2Ch.xxiii.17,17;

ὁ Βααλίμ, Ju.x.10;

οἱ Βααλίμ, Ju.ii.11,iii.7,viii.33,x.6, 1S.xii.10, 1K.xviii.18,xxii.53(54), 2Ch.xxiii.3, xxxiv.4, Hos.ii.17, xi.2;

αἱ Βααλίμ, 1S.vii.4, 2Ch.xxiv.7;

while they express also 'the Baal' in 1K.xviii.19,25, Jer.iii.24, Hos.ix.10, by ἡ αἰσχύνη, 'the shame,' (= בֹּשֶׁת, *bosheth*, as in Ish-bosheth, Mephi-bosheth, Jerubbesheth, *comp*. 'the Bosheth' used for 'the Baal' in Jer.iii.24, xi.13, Hos.ix.10,) and 'the Baalim' by τὰ εἴδωλα, 'the idols,' in 2Ch.xvii.3, xxviii.3(?), Jer.ix.14.

Assyrian colonists with strange religions, yet the worship of JHVH, however adulterated and degenerated, still prevailed there. The writer of 2K.xvii, although very inimically disposed towards that people [the Samaritans], who gave the Jews so much trouble after the Captivity, cannot deny this; see expressly *v*.26–28.[18] If this was so in Ephraim, with surrounding [heathen] tribes, how much more must it have been the case in Judah, which for a long while had not been so much mixed up with Canaanites, and in which, as appears by the result, Mosaism had struck much deeper root than in the north of the land.[19]

[18] The writer of 2K.xvii does not appear to have lived *after*, but *during*, the Captivity, *comp*.2K.xxv.27–30, and therefore had no experience of the 'trouble' which the Samaritans gave the Jews in Nehemiah's time, nor, consequently, had he any special 'animosity' against them. He depicts, indeed, their idolatries very strongly in 2K.xvii; but just as the Deuteronomist paints in the strongest colours the abominations of the Canaanites, and their (imaginary) extermination by Israel under Joshua at God's command, in order to convey a lesson to the people of Judah, and impress upon them the terrible dangers which threatened them in consequence of their own sins: see *P*.III.884–886.

But the language used in 2K.xvii, and especially in *v*.26–28, 'they know not the manner of the God of the land,' seems to point exactly to such a worship of JHVH as we have supposed, which these Assyrian foreigners were taught by one of the former *priests* of JHVH, *v*.27,28, yet were allowed to mingle with it their own idolatrous worships, *v*.29–32: so 'they feared JHVH, and served their own gods,' *v*.33.

[19] What sign have we of Mosaism 'striking' any such 'deep root' in Judah till the time of David and Solomon, some centuries after the Exodus? None whatever. Rather, Samuel, the first great Reformer of Israel, was himself (to all appearance) a man of Ephraim (*P*.V.272), and from his nearer proximity to the Syro-Phœnician tribes may have been brought into closer contact with the higher mysteries of their religion, and among them with the secret meaning of the name JHVH, that name 'full of mystery,' and 'taught in the priestly mysteries by the very oldest Phœnician hierophants,' *P*.V.*App*.III.48.

Instead, therefore, of saying, that from the first 'Mosaism had struck much deeper root in Judah' than in Israel, we should rather say that the influence of Samuel, and of the prophets of his school under David and Solomon, had naturally produced a stronger effect upon Judah, because their force was concentrated, in David's and Solomon's time, around the Court and Sanctuary in Jerusalem. Yet even this must be said with some reservation, when we reflect upon the gross idolatries which were practised all along in Judah even by Solomon himself, and down to the seventeenth year of the *good* king Josiah. The *history*, indeed, is more severe upon the doings

23. With our eye on this fact that, from the time of Solomon onwards, JHVH was incontestably the God of Israel, and observing that 'no people changes its God,' we ask—If in the days of Moses Baal was the national Deity of Israel, when did that complete revolution in the national character take place, by which it became, from the people of Baal, the people of JHVH? If in David's time Baal was still the true God of Israel, what happened, then, through which in Solomon's time, and ever afterwards, JHVH took his place?[20]

of the people of *Israel*: but we must not forget that it was written by a man of *Judah*, and that we have no accounts of the affairs of the northern kingdom from one of themselves, except, perhaps, in the legendary stories of Elijah and Elisha, and except also what we may gather from the prophets who prophesied in Israel, Hosea and Amos, and whose language concerning their countrymen is hardly more strong than that which Jeremiah uses of Judah.

[20] We answer this question in the words of Von der ALM, i.*p*.483 :—'The whole 300 years of the period of the Judges must be regarded as a time, during which the Hebrews and Canaanites, under various leavening influences, were blended into one people. In this process the Israelites, it is true, had the upper hand as regards external power: but, as happens to all conquerors, they submitted themselves to the old inhabitants of the land in respect of religion, morals, and customs. When they came forward as one people under David and Solomon, their whole worship was Phœnician: Phœnicians built the Temple at Jerusalem, and the national Deity became the mysterious Phœnician IAO or JHVH.'

In 'the days of Moses'—or, rather, in 'the days of the Exodus'—there was, as we suppose, *no* national Deity of Israel. What worship they had was loose and undefined, as that of a straggling, undisciplined, horde might be: and thus it had no hold upon them. But, whatever it was, they appear (even from the Bible accounts) to have adopted readily the religion of Canaan, and fell into the worship of the 'God of the land,' the Phœnician Baal, JHVH or IAO. In Samuel's time, JHVH or, as the Prophet desired to have it, JEHOVAH was formally recognised as the 'God of Israel'; and, regarded in this light, there was no strong repugnance in pious minds,—at least, down to the early part of David's reign,—to call JEHOVAH 'the Baal' of Israel,—as we see by the names of the sons of Saul, and Jonathan, and David himself, Eshbaal, Meribbaal, Baalyadah. Thus in the time of Samuel, Saul, and even the early part of David's reign, JEHOVAH was 'the Baal,' even in the eyes of enlightened men, as JHVH *always* was in the eyes of the multitude. There was, therefore, no such 'complete revolution in the national character,' as Dr. OORT speaks of. But very soon, it would seem, in the reign of David,—perhaps, after the erection of the Tabernacle on Mount Zion,—the name 'the Baal' ceased to be used by pious people in speaking of 'JEHOVAH'; it was reserved by them for JHVH, as worshipped by the idolatrous majority. These latter, however,—

24. The circumstance, that in later time JHVH was the 'God of Israel,' is of so great weight, that we have a right *à priori* to assume that he was this from the time when Israel became a people, *i.e.* after the Exodus out of Egypt.[21] Incontestably certain evidences must be adduced to prove the contrary, if we are to be required to believe it.[22]

that is, the people at large—seem certainly to have been in the habit of addressing JHVH by the name 'the Baal,' as we gather from Hos.ii.16,17.

[21] Surely, there is no real evidence in the history (not including, of course, the Pentateuch and Book of Joshua) that Israel did become a people till the days of Samuel. Everything seems to point to Samuel as the great *Organizer*, as well as *Reformer*, of his people : *comp.*1S.vii.3–17, especially *v.*15–17, and 1S.viii,xii. Before his time, as we gather from the accounts in the Judges, they acted as separate tribes,—coming together, voluntarily, Ju.xx.1, but not recognising any central authority, 'doing every man that which was right in his own eyes,' Ju.xxi.25. According to the Song of Deborah, several of the tribes—as Reuben, Gilead, Dan, Asher,—took no part in Barak's great movement, nor are Judah, Simeon, Levi, named in connection with it. So Gideon and Jephthah had only partial followings. Saul seems to have been the first, who summoned with a voice of authority 'all Israel' to war, and 'blew the trumpet throughout all the land, saying, Let the Hebrews hear!' 1S.xiii.3.

In fact, they may more properly be said to have become a nation first, when 'they refused to obey the voice of Samuel, and said, Nay ! but we will have a *king* over us, that we also may be like all the nations, and that our king may judge us, and go out before us, and fight our battles,' 1S.viii.19,20.

[22] The proofs, which seem to show that JHVH was not recognised as the national 'God of Israel' until the days of Samuel—though they had probably before this begun to worship him, as the 'God of the land'—are chiefly the following.

(i) The Elohist distinctly states that the name JHVH was not known in Israel until the time of the Exodus. If we set aside, as unhistorical, the account of the miraculous revelation of this name to Moses, the residual fact, which seems to lie really at the basis of this account, is this, that they did not know that name until they left Egypt and settled in Canaan.

(ii) This is supported by the fact that the Syro-Phœnicians, living in the North of Canaan, in Byblus and on Lebanon, notoriously did use a name, represented in Greek by the same letters as JHVH, *viz.* IAΩ, as the great mysterious name of this Baal, the Sun-God, who was called also 'Adonis' and 'God Most High,' as JEHOVAH is called in Scripture 'Adonai' and 'El Most High.' *P.V.App.*III.10,11, &c.

(iii) It is still further confirmed by the fact that the sacred name IAO, which the Hebrews must have known and used, if they adopted this worship, as they did all other worships of the tribes around them,—(and, in fact, we know they *did* adopt it at some time or other in their history, since we read of women 'weeping for Tammuz,' Ez.viii.14, where Tammuz is another name for Adonis, Mov.i.195),—is not mentioned

25. Some facts, indeed, are quoted to show that, in the worship of Israel, Baal had formerly the place of honour. But we shall see presently that these facts are not sufficient to prove this. First, however, we observe that, while stress is laid on all these, the truly overwhelming number of indications to the contrary is left out of consideration. The whole O.T. agrees in this, that, after the deliverance out of Egypt, in the wilderness of Sinai, a covenant was made between JHVH and Israel —*in other words*, that JHVH *was then adopted as the national God of Israel.*[23]

26. It is true, it may be maintained that this is the work of the Compiler of our Books.[24] But, besides the historical data,

at all among the names of heathen deities, as Moloch, Chemosh, Rimmon, &c. which were the objects of worship among them. This implies that this *name* was not regarded as *idolatrous*, but had been consecrated by being used—as we suppose, first in Samuel's time—as the special name of the 'God of Israel.'

(iv) It is again confirmed by the fact that, whereas the Elohist lived in the days of Samuel, and the other writers of Genesis (except the Deuteronomist) in the days of Saul, David, and Solomon, we find them using 'Jehovah' more and more freely as the age comes lower.

(v) Add, also, that *before* Samuel's time very few—if any—Hebrew names exist, which are compounded with 'Jehovah'—that *in* his time we find names compounded with 'Elohim,' 'Baal,' *and* 'Jehovah,'—that *after* his time names with 'Baal' soon disappear altogether, while those with 'Jehovah' become very numerous.

(vi) Lastly, the phenomena observed in the Psalms (*P.V.App.*II.52,53) seem to us very strongly confirmatory of the above view.

[23] It is true, no doubt, that 'the whole O.T. agrees in this'—*i.e.* in assuming that JHVH was adopted *in the wilderness* as the Covenant-God of Israel. But this was based, as we suppose, upon the story in the Exodus as originally written, and is abundantly explained by the circumstances of their history, as we conceive it. The fact, that there is a consensus of Scripture-writers, asserting or assuming this 'adoption of JHVH' from the Mosaic age, no more suffices to prove the reality of the event itself, than their equally strong asseverations as to the original *purity* of the worship in Israel—'the kindness of her youth,' the 'love of her espousals,' Jer.ii.2, Ez.xvi.8, Hos.ii.15—suffice to prove that they really did 'go after Jehovah in the wilderness,' that 'Israel was holiness unto Jehovah, the firstfruits of His increase.' In short, we appeal to Dr. Oort's own remarks in (4,5) against his argument here: and, indeed, he himself feels the force of this objection, and proceeds to support his view by other reasonings, which appear to us equally unconvincing.

[24] Not of the *Compiler*, but of the *original Writers*, of the story in the Pentateuch —the Elohist and his disciples or immediate followers, as well as the later Deutero-

many of which probably were recorded in a late age, there exists a considerable number of ancient memorials, which show us that, from the time of Moses onward, JHVH was the National God of Israel.[25]

27. Out of the days of Moses himself we have not much that can be literally called genuine; but still we have somewhat. We shall not make any use of the superscription to the Decalogue, 'I am JHVH thy Elohim,' since that may be disputed.[26] But, apart from this, the refrain of the hymn, E.xv.1,2, is most probably genuine, and there we have 'Sing ye JHVH!'[27] The same Divine Name is mentioned also in the old war-song against Amalek, E.xvii.16,—

'The hand on the banner of JAH! War of JHVH against Amalek for ever!'[28]

28. So, too, there is no reason why N.x.35,36 should not be nomist. For all these wrote, as we suppose, at a time when the name JHVH was already used in Israel, and recognised (as we suppose it first began to be under Samuel) as the name of the God of Israel.

[25] This, of course, is a statement of great importance, if only it can be confirmed by facts. The reader's attention is requested especially to this point,—that is, to Dr. Oort's evidences in support of his assertion, and to our notes upon them.

[26] Dr. Oort is right in saying that the argument from the occurrence of 'JHVH thy Elohim' in E.xx.2,5,7,10,12, 'may be disputed.' For there can be little doubt that the Decalogue in its *earlier* form, E.xx.2–17, as well as in its *later*, D.v.6–21, is due to the Deuteronomist. See *App.*I.

[27] Prof. KUENEN, who originally (*Eng. Ed.* p.106) regarded E.xv.1–18 as a 'genuine Mosaic song,' has since written to me (*p.*107), 'This seems to me now too conservative: I cannot deny that you have made the Mosaic origin of this song appear much more doubtful.' It appears to me, in fact, to be due—as are all the poetical pieces in Genesis (*P.V.Anal.*337,xxxviii.N.B.)—to the Jehovist of the age of David.

[28] What *proof* is there, of any kind, to show that this utterance is Mosaic? Why may not this declaration of internecine war against Amalek be also due to the Jehovist, writing at a time when the atrocities of the Amalekites, committed against Israel, were recently committed—when they had 'invaded the south, and smitten Ziklag, and burned it with fire, and had taken the women captives that were therein. . . And David and his men came to the city, and behold! it was burned with fire; and their wives and their sons and their daughters were taken captives. And David and the people that were with him lifted up their voice and wept, until they had no more power to weep,' 1S.xxx.1–4—and expressing the savage feelings of the people against these insolent invaders?

Mosaic.²⁹ It contains two short addresses to JHVH, upon the setting-forth and resting of the Ark: in any case, therefore, it dates from the time when this Sanctuary was carried about in war,³⁰ of which we find no more trace after David's age. These are—

> 'Arise, JHVH! let thine enemies be scattered,
> Let them that hate Thee flee before Thee!'
> 'Return, JHVH, to* the ten-thousands of the tribes of Israel!'

29. The same conclusion may be drawn, if we examine the memorials out of the times of the Judges. For instance, the title of a certain document in which, among other matters, there were recorded conflicts out of the Mosaic time, is 'The Book of the Wars of JHVH,' N.xxi.14.³¹ So the 'Song of Deborah'

---

²⁹ I have shown in *App*.II. that this passage is, in all probability, a Deuteronomistic interpolation.

³⁰ This does not seem to follow at all. The passage in question, N.x.33-36, does not refer to the Ark being taken out to *war*, but speaks merely of ordinary marches in the wilderness. And surely it would not have required any great effort of imagination to have invented such formulæ as these in a later day,—especially, as the first of them was adapted, as we suppose, from Ps.lxviii.1?

³¹ It is very doubtful if this 'Book of the Wars of JHVH' did record 'conflicts out of the Mosaic time.' It is only mentioned in this one place of the Bible, and the extract here made from it does not appear to have any connection with the affairs of Israel at the time of the Exodus. It is true, the *Eng. Vers.* would seem to imply the contrary—'What He did *at the Red Sea*, &c.' But this translation is unquestionably wrong. The LXX has τὴν Ζωὸβ ἐφλόγισε, 'set-on-fire Zahab,' having evidently read אֶת־זָהָב for אֶת־וָהֵב: *comp.* מִי־זָהָב, *Me-zahab*, the name of an ancient Edomitish chief, G.xxxvi.39. KNOBEL retains the usual reading, but renders the passage thus:—

> 'Vaheb in Suphah,
> And the brooks of Arnon;
> And the stream of the brooks,
> Which descendeth to the dwelling of Ar,
> And leaneth upon the border of Moab.'

And he observes that the quotation is abrupt, the verb being left out at the beginning, *e.g.* 'they (the Amorites) possessed,' *i.e.* as their southern border. But, at all events, the form of the Hebrew expressions shows plainly that we have in

---

* Or, 'Return, Thou ten-thousand, &c.!' according to 2K.ii.12. E. MEIER, *Gesch. der Poet. Nation. der Hebr.*, p.48, adds to these Mosaic documents also N.vi.24-26; but the genuineness of this may be contested.—OORT.

distinctly declares that JHVH was the 'God of Israel,' in whose Name the tribes were summoned to war; the war against the Canaanites was a war of JHVH, v.23, and the people is called the 'people of JHVH,' v.11.[32]

30. It is true, men may shrug the shoulder and say, 'Yes! but who knows how much has been changed in it in later days?' It may be maintained that the Rabbies, who allowed themselves some liberties with Proper Names to which they had an objection, may have everywhere set JHVH in place of Baal. But, certainly, they were not so free as this in their changes. The varying traditions and legends out of the time of the Judges show how much they left unchanged which must have been displeasing to them.[33]

---

the first word the name of a place, such as Vaheb (or Zahab). He adds also, ii. p.114, that 'Suphah' appears to be the name of a place; and in Arabic tho word means *terra mollis inter duram et arenosam*, 'soft land in the midst of hard and sandy,' and actually appears as the name of a place, *Maraszid*, ii.p.68, though not in the locality here meant.

KEIL and DELITZSCH, in their very orthodox commentary, while maintaining that the 'Book of the Wars of JHVH' was 'a collection of songs out of the time of Moses,' yet remark, ii.p.286, '*Vaheb* is without doubt the name of an Amoritish fortress, and בְּסוּפָה, *bĕsuphah*, means 'in a storm,' as in Nah.i.3'; and so they render the passage 'He took Vaheb in a storm, &c.,' understanding 'He' to mean 'JHVH.' But there is nothing whatever to decide this. The subject of the verb understood *may* have been JHVH, or it may have been *Moses, Israel, Joshua*, the *Amorite*, or even *David*. At all events, if this 'Book' was written (as we suppose) in David's days, the title is at once explained; since in that age JHVH was the covenant-God who fought for Israel, Ps.lxviii.4,16,18,20. See *App*.V.14,16.

[32] We believe the 'Song of Deborah' to be also a poem out of the Davidic age, and imitated in part from Ps.lxviii. KEIL and DELITZSCH observe, iii.p.234—'This highly poetical song is so direct and lively an expression of the glowing energy of the spirit which was called forth by the mighty exaltation of Israel and the victory gained over Sisera, that its genuineness at the present day is generally recognised.' But surely this assumes an utter absence of the poetical spirit in Israel,—as if it was not possible for a later poet—*e.g.* one writing under the influence of the 'glowing energy' of David's time—to *imagine* such a state of things as that here pictured, and to produce such a poem as this,—as Lord Macaulay in his 'Lays of Ancient Rome,' and Burns in his 'Scots wha hae wi' Wallace bled,' have thrown themselves into the spirit of earlier ages. See *App*.III.

[33] From our point of view we do not need any of these later Rabbinical alterations. We suppose that *generally*, throughout the Pentateuch and the whole Bible,

31. All the narratives in Judges and Samuel * mention JHVH as the tribal Deity of Israel;[34] and these are for a great part very old, and we have them preserved pretty much in their original form. It is plain, for instance, that the account of Jephthah's sacrificing his daughter to JHVH cannot have been written at a time, when the sacrifice of a human being was deemed unlawful.[35]

[corrected] JHVH stands now where it was first written; though we believe also that the first-written passage, in which it occurs, E.vi.2-7, was written in the age of Samuel.

But, while we heartily agree with Dr. OORT's judgment as to the improbability of the Rabbies having made such numerous changes, we apply also this principle to confirm our own argument (*P.V.App.*II.52,53), that, where Elohim and Jehovah occur in the Second Book of the Psalms, they were most probably so written by the original writer or writers. It seems to us highly improbable that the original 'Jehovah' in these Psalms should have been changed by some later hand into 'Elohim,'—much more, that they should have been changed so arbitrarily and irregularly, as to have left 'Jehovah' still standing, *once, twice, thrice,* or *four* times in different Psalms. But if the prevalent use of 'Elohim,' which singularly characterises these Psalms, is really due to their writer or writers, there must have been a reason for this, which our view supplies, by supposing that the Name 'Jehovah' had only been recently introduced into the worship of devout men, as that of the God of Israel, when these Psalms were written,—*some* of them certainly, as we believe, as Ps.lx and Ps.lxviii—if not *all*—in the reign of David.

[34] Why should they not do this, since, however old, they were written *after* the time, when JHVH had been adopted as the 'God of Israel' in Samuel's age? This, at least, is our view, though we cannot, of course, give the full proof of it, without going through the whole Book of Judges. But we have given reasons in *App*. III for concluding that Ju.v is of the age of David; and Ju.xvii-xxi is shown to be also not earlier than the time of Saul, from the repeated mention of the fact that 'in those days there was no king in Israel,' xvii.6, xviii.1, xix.1, xxi.25. Again, Prof. KUENEN says, *Hist. Krit. Onderzoek*, i.p.212, that 'the Book of Jasher (Book of the Righteous), from which Ju.iv.4-24 is derived, was composed *in* or *after* David's reign, and that the full account of the wars of the Philistines, from which Ju.xiii-xvi is derived, cannot be older than David, and is most probably much younger; and so, too, the documents used in Ju.vi-ix, were certainly as far from being contemporary with the events referred to, as that from which the writer derived the history of Jephthah, Ju.xi.1-xii.6.' See also *App*. IV.

Lastly, some portions appear to be interpolations by the Deuteronomistic Editor.

[35] But Dr. OORT himself has shown, *het Menschenoffer in Israel*, that there is no

* I take no account of *Joshua*, because this Book was brought into its present shape at a very late date, and it is almost impossible to recognise anywhere the oldest form of its contents.—OORT.

32. The legend of Samson, with the lifelong Nazariteship in honour of JHVH, which is therein mentioned and dignified, is very far indeed from showing a priestly or prophetical, much less a rabbinical, colour.[36] Ju.xvii gives us a view of a JHVH-istic worship, the account of which has certainly not been recorded or retouched by orthodox Israelites; for it tends to the glorification of the famous sanctuary at Dan, which was not exactly to their taste.[37]

33. If the Sanctuary at Shiloh was a temple of Baal, how, then, can we explain the origin of the accounts in 1S.i–iii? These accounts are ancient; for the true priest, whom JHVH will raise up instead of the house of Eli, ii.35, can be no other than Zadok;* and this narrative, therefore, must have been composed shortly after Solomon's time,[38] when the house of

---

sign that human sacrifices were condemned as wicked, even by good men, in the time of David or long afterwards. We believe that the account of Abraham's intended sacrifice in G.xxii was written in David's age, with a view, indeed, of discouraging the practice, but yet *commending* it, as emanating from a holy and Divine impulse, and certainly *not condemning* it.

[36] True. But why may not the legend of Samson have been written in the age of David, after the many conflicts with the Philistines, which Israel had had in the days of Saul and David? In fact, as we have seen (note [34]), Prof. KUENEN says that this narrative 'cannot be older than David, and is most probably much younger.'

[37] True, again. But such an account might have been written in David's time, or even afterwards, before the separation of the two kingdoms, and the establishment of the calf-worship by Jeroboam at Dan. And we have given reasons (*P.*II.463) for believing that Ju.xviii.30 was interpolated at a still later time.

[38] The account in 1S.i–iii may have been written *during the latter part of Solomon's reign*, in order to justify the conduct of Solomon in expelling the aged Abiathar, and putting Zadok in his room, 1K.ii.35.

Dr. OORT, however, supposes that it was written '*after* Solomon's time,'— that is, *two centuries* after the time to which it refers. And some part of it, at all events, must be 'explained as a mere fiction,' *e.g.* Hannah's Song, ii.1–10, which is manifestly, as we have said, a Psalm of later date, and quite unsuited in some respects to her circumstances. It is, therefore, very difficult to say how much of the whole narrative can be regarded as really historical. It is written

* THENIUS explains this, quite incorrectly, of Samuel, *Sam.p.*14. But Samuel was honoured as a *prophet*, not as a *priest*. That he discharged priestly offices is, of course, true; for so did, in those days, any one that would.—OORT.

Zadok had obtained the chief priestly distinctions in the Temple. All that we learn further about the worship at Shiloh, ii.13,22, iii.3, is so little in the spirit of the later priestly institutions, that it can hardly be explained here as a mere fiction.

34. It seems to me that these facts, to which many others might be added, place *this* above all doubt,—that from the time of Moses onward JHVH was the national God of Israel, so that every one, who would bear the name of Israelite, must be a JHVH-worshipper.[39]

35. Let us now consider what weight is to be attached to the proofs, which Dr. Dozy has produced out of the O.T., to show that Baal occupied in ancient times the place which was after-

throughout in the style and tone of a later time, and employs the name 'Jehovah' almost exclusively. But the accounts of the misconduct of Eli's sons very probably contain a reminiscence of the character of the ancient worship at Shiloh, and show that it was loose, impure, and disorderly—the worship of JHVH rather than JEHOVAH.

There is, however, no real proof that JHVH was actually worshipped in Eli's days at Shiloh. It is true, the name 'Jehovah' is employed very freely in the story. But so, too, the Jehovistic parts of Genesis represent the patriarchs as praying to Jehovah, and Jehovah as answering and appearing to them; whereas the Elohist plainly tells us that they did not know Him by this Name. There was, no doubt, an ancient Sanctuary at Shiloh, perhaps contemporary with the settlement of the Israelites in Canaan. But the question is whether they worshipped there *from the first* with the name JHVH, having learnt it from Moses in the wilderness, or whether they learnt the use of this name gradually from the tribes of Canaan, and used at first more familiarly the names 'Elohim,' 'El Shaddai,' 'Adonai,' as, according to the Elohist, the patriarchs did. This latter seems to be indicated by the total absence—or at least the great paucity—of names compounded with JHVH before the time of Samuel, and the existence of so many names in that age compounded with El, as Othni*el*, *El*imelech, *El*kanah, *El*ihu, Samu*el*, *El*eazar, with the multitude of similar names in the Pentateuch itself, II.301,302, most probably from the hand of the Jehovist in David's days. That they also used 'Baal' is probable from our finding of such names as Jerub*baal*, *Baal*, 1Ch.ix.36, and Esh*baal*, Merib*baal*, *Baal*yadah, *Baal*iah, *Baal*hanan, in the time of Saul and David.

[39] I should rather state the residual historical fact, which is 'placed above all doubt,' as follows: As from the time of the entrance of Israel in Canaan they must have come into contact with the Name JHVH, so from the time of Samuel onward, and chiefly by his influence, JHVH became the popular name of the God of Israel, so that, &c.

wards taken by JHVH.⁴⁰ He argues first from the name Kirjath-Baal and from Am.v.25,26, that the Ark and Tabernacle were in reality Sanctuaries of Baal.⁴¹ Let us see what can be made out from these particulars.

36. The place where the Ark stood, after having been some time in the hands of the Philistines, was called Baal or Kirjath-Baal (city of Baal), afterwards Kirjath-Jearim (city of forests), Jo.xv.9,10, xviii.14. The change of name took place after David's time,—perhaps, long afterwards, since the writer of 2S.vi.2 says merely, 'David went to Baal of Judah,' without the addition, 'that is Kirjath-Jearim,' which the Chronicler adds, 1Ch.xiii.6. It is nowhere mentioned, however, that the town Kirjath-Baal was so named, because the Ark stood there; and the names of places compounded with Baal are so numerous that probably we ought not to assume this.⁴²

37. On the contrary, the name 'Baal of Judah' sounds as if the writer of 1Samuel found nothing very strange in this expression, and regarded the use of the name in that instance as quite on a par with what had happened in other cases. Thus there was a 'Baal' or 'Baal of the Well' in Simeon, 1Ch.iv.33, Jo.xix.8 (Dozy, *p.*87,88), 'Baal of Gad,' Jo.xi.17, xii.7, 'Baal-Perazim,' 2S.v.20, 1Ch.xiv.11, 'Baal-Meon,' N.xxxii.38, 1Ch.v.8,

---

⁴⁰ Our view is midway between those of Dozy and Oort. We believe that JHVH did not 'take the place' of the Baal, but was itself the great mysterious Name of the Syro-Phœnician Baal, which was adopted in Samuel's time as the great name of the God of Israel. In the eyes of the multitude, all along, down to the time of the Captivity, it was only the name of their own particular Baal or Lord, the 'God of the land' which they had conquered and called their own: though a few nobler minds in every age used it in a higher, more spiritual, sense, as the Name of the Lord of Lords, the Living God above all Gods, D.x.17, Jo.xxii.22.

⁴¹ According to our view, the Ark and Tabernacle became Sanctuaries of JHVH in the people's eyes, *because* they were Sanctuaries of the Baal; and the great and good in each age tried to purify the worship of JHVH into that of Jehovah.

⁴² It is no part of *our* theory to assume this. But the occurrence of so many of these names shows that the worship of the Baal was very common in the towns of Canaan, either *before* the arrival of the Israelites, or *after* it, as appears to be indicated by the Proper Names compounded with Baal (note ⁴⁰), as well as by the expressions 'Baal of Judah,' 'Baal of Gad,' &c. (note ⁹).

Ez.xxv.9, 'Baal-Shalisha,' 2K.iv.42, 'Baal-Tamar,' Ju.xx.33, 'Baal-Hamon,' Cant.viii.11. In later days the 'Baal' was removed out of all these names, and so we find '*Beth*-Meon,' Jer.xlviii.23, '*Beth*-Tamar,' '*Beth*-Shalisha,' &c. (See *Bijb. Woord. voor het Chr. gezin* on these articles.)

There is, consequently, not the least reason to suppose that Kirjath-Baal was so named because of the Ark.[43]

38. And now let us look at Am.v.25,26. Dr. Dozy translates the passage thus:—

'Have ye brought to Me sacrifices and gifts in the wilderness forty years long, O House of Israel? Nay! ye carried the tent of your King, and Chiun your idol, the star of your God, which ye had made.'

He considers that Chiun or Chivan is the same as Saturn, *i.e.* Baal. And from this passage it follows, according to his view, that the Tabernacle mentioned in the Pentateuch was a Baal-Temple, and that no public JHVH-worship existed.

39. The conclusion which Prof. Dozy has drawn from this passage I can only regard as extravagant. If we assume for a moment that his reading and translation are correct, we stumble at once on these difficulties. In the first place, mention is made here not of *one* object, but of *three*,—*viz.* a *Tent*, a *Chiun*, a *Star*,—or of *two* objects, if we join the last two; for we read

[43] We agree entirely with this conclusion of Dr. OORT. But it may be observed that the form of the name Kirjath-Baal differs from that in the other instances. In those we have 'Baal of &c.' = 'Lord of &c.,' referring, apparently, to the particular shrine or temple of Baal in that place,—as we have in modern times 'Our Lady of Loretto,' &c. But Kirjath-Baal means 'city of Baal,' and implies that the town was especially consecrated to Baal, as Ephesus was the 'city of Diana,' Athens 'of Athene,' &c. Perhaps, many of these names may have existed before the Hebrews settled in Canaan, (*comp.* Kirjath-Arba, Kirjath-Sepher,) and the places may have been only *adopted* by them as sacred places. In that case, instead of Kirjath-Baal having been so called from the Ark, it may have been that the Ark—whatever kind of Ark it was—may, when brought back from the Philistines, have been first taken to 'Beth-Shemesh,' (House of the *Sun, comp.* Beth-El), 1S.vi.9, as a sacred place, and thence to Kirjath-Baal, 1S.vii.1, *comp.* 2S.vi.2, as a place of yet greater sanctity,—Shiloh having been ravaged or deserted, or at least desecrated as a holy place by the recent events.

here 'the tent of your King *and* Chiun.' In his explanation the conjunction seems to fall away, and the King himself to be called Chiun or Chivan.

40. Again, the name Chivan occurs nowhere else in the O.T. What right have we to identify it with Baal? The reasoning is this: Chivan is 'the planet Saturn'; Baal also is Saturn; and thus Chivan is Baal. But it cannot be proved that Baal was a name of 'the *planet* Saturn'; and, even if this could be shown, it is still certain that the Israelites did not know this; and therefore the language of Amos, if it referred to the Baal-worship, must have been altogether unintelligible to them. We shall return to this point presently.

41. Lastly, 'the Tent (סֻכַּת = סִכּוּת) of your King' is said to be identical with the (so-called) Mosaic Tabernacle; in respect of which it is not observed that the Tabernacle is always called in the Pentateuch אֹהֶל, *ohel*, or מִשְׁכָּן, *mishkan*, and [סֹךְ=]סֻכַּת, *sukkath*, only once, in poetry, Ps.lxxvi.3.

42. Hitherto, however, we have been assuming that Dr. Dozy's translation is correct. But this is subject to several objections.

(i) The stress in the Hebrew is not laid upon *Me*, as in the translation.

(ii) The parallelism is disturbed by making 'your image' stand *in apposition to* 'Chiun,' of which it seems rather to be a *definition*.

(iii) The pointing of 'Chiun' is changed into *Cheivan*, whereas Chiun (= κιὼν, 'pillar' *) is capable of other explanations.

(iv) It is arbitrary also to change the plural, 'your images,' into the singular.

(v) Lastly, it may be questioned if the conjunction in *v*.26 can denote 'Nay! on the contrary, &c.'

43. Probably Prof. Dozy would not have explained the passage thus, if he had read it over in connection with what precedes and follows. For this is just what, according to him, the prophet says:

'I, JHVH, hate your sacrifices, and all external worship: rather, be doing righteousness. Did you bring me sacrifices in the wilderness? Nay! then you served idols: therefore I will carry you into captivity.'

---

* See Hitzig *in loco*. If the words, 'the Star of your God,' are genuine, (which some doubt,) then they express what is to be understood by 'Chiun.' If they are not genuine, then they contain the oldest *commentary* upon it.—Oort.

It is obvious that there is a fault here in the argument.

44. *Has* Amos here ascribed idolatry to the Israelites of the time of Moses? This is very doubtful; and one must be somewhat imaginative before one can find this in it. Prof. HOEKSTRA (*Godg. Bijdr.* 1863, *p.*89,90) has long ago struck into another path; he gives this explanation:—

'Did you sacrifice to me in the wilderness, and (at the same time) serve your idols (as you do now)? Truly, I will carry you away into captivity.'

The answer, that must be understood to the question, would then be, 'No! *then* Israel served JHVH alone.'

Here, however, the words of the original must be supplied by inserting 'at the same time' and 'as you do now,' and this indeed, presents some difficulty,—still much less than if we suppose that the idolatry of Israel in the wilderness is here described.

45. Various other explanations have been given (*comp.* O. BAUR, *der Prophet Amos erklärt*, *p.*364–379.) But the passage is too obscure for me to maintain any one of them without limitation. Whatever Amos, however, may have meant by it, this is certain, at all events, that we have no right to appeal to his words in support of the view, that Israel began with a worship of Baal, and the Tabernacle was a Sanctuary of Baal, unless it can be shown distinctly that this can be read here.[44]

---

[44] We agree generally with Dr. OORT's remarks on this passage, but with some slight modification. The Prophet seems to reason thus: 'Did you offer to me in the wilderness sacrifices and offerings *forty years long*, O House of Israel?—and yet—after all this—you carried the Tabernacle of your King, &c.!' The stress is not here laid on the words 'to me,' as if the contrast was between the worship of Jehovah and the worship of idols; but the Prophet assumes the general truth of the Pentateuchal story of their having been led *forty years* by Jehovah through the wilderness, receiving daily blessings from Him, and offering daily worship to Him;—and now after all this experience of His goodness, and long-continued expression of dependence upon Him, they have become gross idolaters!

According to this, the words of Amos *assume* an orthodox Jehovah-worship in the wilderness, and a subsequent falling-away to idolatry—how soon is not said.

46. The 'Tabernacle' was no Sanctuary of Baal. What was it then? a Sanctuary dedicated to JHVH? In the sense which is usually given to the word 'Sanctuary,' so that the first thought is of a place for sacrifices and public worship, the 'Tabernacle of Meeting' [E.V. 'the congregation'] was certainly not this. How strong the power of tradition is, appears again manifestly from the manner in which the argument is carried on about this Tabernacle. In E.xxv-xxvii a *portable* Sanctuary is described; and, that this representation is of much later date, is certain. Yet, involuntarily, whenever we read in Exodus and Numbers of a 'Tabernacle of Meeting,' we think at once of such a construction. Into this mistake even Prof. Dozy falls,[45] when he speaks of the Ark 'which stood in the Holy of Holies.'

This, in fact, corresponds with the usual traditional view, as gathered from the Pentateuch and Book of Judges.
The 'Tent of their King' is certainly not to be identified with the 'Mosaic Tabernacle'; for the latter was an imaginary construction, copied probably from the details of the Temple of Solomon, and the former was a reality.

[45] Does not Dr. OORT himself seem to feel the 'power of tradition,' when he assumes the real existence of a 'Mosaic Tabernacle' at all? If the elaborate account in E.xxv-xxvii must be set aside, as he says,—and as it undoubtedly must—as being of much later date than the time of Moses, what is to guarantee to us the historical value of the earlier datum in E.xxxiii.7? May not this also express only the idea of a somewhat earlier age, as to what the people *might be supposed to have had* in the wilderness under Moses, rather than describe what they actually had?
On the other hand, *both* these accounts, critically considered, may contain real history. For they may give us an idea of what really existed in Israel at the times when these passages were written,—of what the writers had had before their eyes, or of what was still retained in the recollection of their contemporaries. Thus the account in E.xxxiii.7 may shadow forth the state of things at Shiloh in Samuel's time, or at Nob in Saul's time: while E.xxv-xxvii may be due to the age of Solomon, and give us some idea of the construction, not only of Solomon's Temple of Jerusalem, but of Hiram's Temple also, built for the Tyrian Hercules at Tyre, from which Solomon's is believed to have been copied.
Prof. DOZY's expression, therefore, may not be altogether a mistake, inasmuch as the Ark, to whatever Deity dedicated, would, no doubt, be placed in the most sacred recess—the Holy of Holies—of the Tabernacle, whatever may have been its construction.

47. If, setting aside this (probably) post-Exilic[46] representation, we read the oldest notices about the Mosaic Sanctuary, E.xxxiii.7, &c., we shall see that nothing is said here about a public place of prayer. The 'Tabernacle of Meeting' was (what the name expresses) a Tent of Revelation, the place where JHVH 'met' with Moses.[47] In later times, the 'Tabernacle of Meeting' was regarded as a place to which sacrifices were brought, L.xii,xix; till at last a description of it came into the world, which has very little of a Mosaic character.*[48]

48. If the Tabernacle was not devoted to the worship of Baal, just as little was the Feast at the Gilgal kept to his honour. Whoever reads the passages where this Feast is mentioned, Hos.iv.15,xii.11,Am.iv.4,v.5, will readily perceive this.[49]

---

[46] There seems reason to believe from the researches of POPPER, *der Bibl. Bericht über die Stiftshütte,* that the account of the *completion* of the Tabernacle in E.xxxv-xl, which is almost a repetition of the directions in E.xxv-xxx, may be of very late date, and, as OORT says, post-Exilic. But at present I believe that the original directions themselves are of the age of Solomon.

[47] Rather, the 'Tabernacle' was the place where Jehovah would meet *any one* who sought Him: *comp.* E.xxv.22,xxix.42,43,xxx.36, N.xvii.4.

[48] Viz. that in E.xxv-xxxiv. Why assume that the original idea has *more* of a '*Mosaic* character,' unless, indeed, the word 'Mosaic' is used of ideas *attributed* in the Pentateuch to Moses, but not therefore necessarily his?

[49] All these passages seem rather to imply that *idolatries,* at all events, were practised at the Gilgal, though the people sware by JHVH — חי־יהוה, 'Life of JHVH!'='JHVH for ever!'—as their king (Malcham): *comp.* 'Life of Pharaoh!' G.xlii.15,16, 'Life of thy soul!' 1S.i.26, xvii.55. In short, they seem all to support the view that JHVH (= IAO), *i.e.* the Syro-Phœnician Baal, was worshipped by the multitude—though not by pious Prophets and Psalmists—at the Gilgal and elsewhere in Judah and Israel.

---

* If the Tabernacle was not a sanctuary of Baal, so neither is Aaron (אהרון) a mythical person, whose name is merely a transposition of the letters of the word הארון, 'the ark,' Dozy, *p.*42. The oldest tradition about him—[what is the value of this, any more than of those about King Arthur, or about Hengist and Horsa, *lit.* 'stallion and mare,' whose existence as *men* is very much doubted?]—condemns this conjecture, since it represents him, not as Priest, but as the *locum-tenens* of Moses. As such he appears with Miriam as early as Micah, vi.4—[that is, *seven centuries* after the Exodus, which may be compared with Hengist and Horsa spoken of in the reign of Henry VII!]—OORT.

Nothing is said there about *idolatry* in the strict sense of the word.[50] In Am.v.5 we read,—

'Seek not Bethel, and come not to the Gilgal, and go not to Beersheba ; for the *Gilgal* shall certainly be carried-captive (גּלה, *galah*), and the House-of-*El* (Beth-El) shall become Vanity (און, *Aven*)' [where there is an allusion to the name of a place near Bethel, Jo.vii.2, 'Beth-Aven,' which name is applied to Bethel itself by the prophet Hosea, iv.15, x.5].

The position here assigned to the Gilgal, in connection with Beersheba and Bethel, where JHVH-worship was practised, forbids us to think of Baal-worship there.[51] On the Gilgal a JHVH-worship was celebrated, though quite as little to the taste of the Prophets as the worship at Bethel and elsewhere.[52]

49. The other facts of the O.T., which are quoted by Professor Dozy, in order to show that even in David's time there existed a worship of Baal, if not ranking above, yet co-ordinate with, the worship of JHVH,[53] are some names of persons com-

[50] That is, nothing is said about the worship of 'the Baal' as *opposed* to that of JHVH, because, when the populace worshipped 'the Baal,' they worshipped JHVH,—though with impure and unbecoming ceremonies. Just so in Zululand, where the Missionaries use the native name for the Deity, 'Unkulunkulu,' as the proper Name for God, they would not condemn the people as *idolaters*—as worshipping *another* God, in opposition to 'Unkulunkulu'—if they found them observing any old heathen ceremonies, when engaged in the worship of Unkulunkulu himself. And, in like manner, a zealous Protestant prophet of our day might condemn the Romish worship as base and even idolatrous, without saying that it was 'idolatry in the strict sense of the word,'—that is, without saying that the Papist, in worshipping God, was worshipping a different Being from the God whom he himself worshipped.

[51] Not so, if that very JHVH-worship was for the masses IAO-worship, that is, Baal-worship.

[52] Exactly so: that is to say, the JHVH-feast, held on the Gilgal, was condemned by the Prophets as an idolatrous IAO-Feast, though they still approved the *name* JHVH, as the recognised name of the God of Israel.

[53] In our view, the Baal-worship in David's time ranked neither *above* nor *with* the JHVH-worship: it was simply identical with it. All the people worshipped JHVH: but some few had purer, more exalted, ideas of the Divine Majesty and Spirituality, while the masses shared the low, gross, notions of the Canaanite tribes around them. Yet even these (let us remember) were not, perhaps, altogether so corrupt and debased, as our modern views of religion might lead us

pounded with Baal. From this fact the Rabbins have drawn such a conclusion; and in order to conceal this discovery, which was anything but agreeable to them, and to erase as much as possible this sorrowful memorial of the olden time, they have changed Baal into Bosheth ('shame') or into El.

50. We, however, ought not to be guilty of a similar fault. The use of the name 'Baal' was no offence in the view of the most zealous worshippers of JHVH in David's time, for this reason, that the name did not exist at all as the name of a Deity who stood in opposition to JHVH.[54] We shall show this more at length in Section II, and will here make only one remark, which raises already this suspicion.

to suppose. The more intelligent Romanists do not actually worship the image or picture before which they bow: they regard it only as the symbol of the Divine. And so too, doubtless, among the tribes of Canaan, there were those, who, while they worshipped the Sun as Life-Giver, or sacrificed to him their best and dearest, (as Abraham in the story was willing to do,) had some confused ideas of the Majesty of Him 'with whom we have to do,' and of the right which He has to claim our best service of 'body, soul, and spirit, which are His.'

We may copy on this point the following passage from *P.V.*382:—

'In fact, the state of Israel may be compared with that which, in the view of many ardent Protestants, exists even now in some Roman-Catholic communities. The people in such cases worship the same God as English Protestants: they call themselves Christians, as servants of the same Lord. Yet there is much in their religion, which not a few English travellers regard as profane and idolatrous, and denounce as gross abominations. The desire, however, of such persons would be, not to teach these (so-called) 'idolaters' to use another name as the name of 'their King,' but to teach them to use the same name worthily. They call them idolaters, not because they bow at the name of Jesus, but because they worship images, adore the Host, and mix up, with the honours due to their one true Lord, the worship of Saints and Virgins innumerable,—which, though, like the Baalim and Ashtaroth of old, supposed to shadow forth under various aspects the glory of the great Life-Giver, have come at last to be regarded as separate divinities, and stand, as such, between the worshipper and the LORD, the Living God.'

Hence also may be explained the fact that, whereas Hezekiah had 'removed the high-places, and shattered the images, and hewn-down the asheras, &c.,' 2K.xviii.4, in his kingdom, Rabshakeh says to the Jews, *v.*22, 'But, if ye say unto me 'We trust in JHVH our Elohim,' is that not He, whose high-places and whose altars Hezekiah hath taken away, &c.?'—for these high-places were really 'high-places of JHVH.'

[54] It need scarcely be repeated that this corresponds precisely with our own view.

51. The only names of persons, that we know of, compounded with Baal (except Jerubbaal, Ju.vi.32) are those of sons of *Saul* [Esh-Baal, 1Ch.viii.33,] and of *David*, [Baalyadah, 1Ch.xiv.7,] and of an officer and a hero of *David*, Baalhanan, 1Ch.xxvii.28, Baaljah, 1Ch.xii.5. This may be accidental; since the notices of other similar names may, perhaps, have been struck out by those who have manipulated these writings. Yet it is remarkable that just in this particular age these names appear in peaceable union with that of JHVH, [*comp.* especially Baal-Jah = JHVH *is* Baal,]—inasmuch as the national strength of Israel had then awaked in great strength, and David, at all events, must have been zealously opposed to everything that was anti-JHVH-istic.*[55]

[55] Add to the above the names of Baal, the brother of Ner, *Saul's* grandfather, 1Ch.ix.36, and of *Jonathan's* son, Meribbaal, 1Ch.ix.40. See also *App*.V.

Dr. OORT's remark, however, entirely accords with our view, that in David's time JHVH had only been recently recognised as the Name of the God of Israel.

Yet it would seem that the *Psalmists* and *Prophets* abstained from using the name 'Baal' in connection with JHVH. At all events, it occurs nowhere in any of their writings except Hos.ii.16,—'Thou shalt call me *Ishi* (my Husband), and shalt call me no more *Baali* (my Lord)'—where there is probably a reference to the name 'Baal,' (as if the people had all along been calling Jehovah 'their Baal,') but also to the *social* position of the *wife*, as contrasted with that of a *servant* or *slave*.

So, again, it is remarkable that in the Pentateuch we have many names compounded with El, but none (except Joshua and Jochebed) compounded with either JHVH or Baal. We may regard the first of these facts as a proof that the name JHVH had not long been used familiarly in the religious worship of Israel, at the time when the passages, including these names, were written, and the second as an indication that the more advanced minds in Israel had already begun to feel a distaste for the use of 'Baal.'

Upon the whole, it would almost seem as if these pious writers preferred to leave 'Baal' to be used for 'Lord,' as the heathen used it, with reference only to the worship of JHVH or IAO; while in the worship of Jehovah they used habitually the synonym 'Adonai.'

---

* The inference, that Baal was a general Divine Name, has been derived from this fact also by Dr. TH. NOLDEKE, *Zeitsch.d.m.G*.xv.*p*.809. Dr. A. GEIGER, who treats of the use of Baal in Proper Names, *Zeitsch.d.m.G*.xvi.728-732, does not determine what conclusion follows from it for the confirmation of the meaning of the name Baal.—OORT.

SECTION II.

MEANING OF THE BAAL AND THE BAALIM.

52. PROF. DOZY writes, *p*.36, as follows:—

The name 'Baal,' or, rather, with the article, 'the Baal,' *i.e.* the Lord, was that of the greatest Deity in a great part of Asia. He was at once the Sun, the planet Saturn, and the planet Mars, *i.e.* (if MOVERS's view is correct) the *producing, sustaining,* and *destroying* power. Here, however, we are only concerned with his meaning as Saturn. As such, he was the highest deity with the Phœnicians and Carthagians, the El *par excellence,* to whom the other Elohim were subordinated.

53. Whence comes this interpretation? It is not enough merely to refer briefly to MOVERS's *Phönizie* I. How does MOVERS come to find that Baal has anything in common with the planet Saturn? In point of fact, the proposition is a mere castle in the air. It derives some countenance from the fact that the Greeks and Romans, who occupied themselves much with Asiatic history and worship, sometimes combined Bel with Kronos or Saturn. This was first done, if the citations of MOVERS, *p*.185, are all that can be produced, three centuries after Christ by SERVIUS *ad Æn.,* who has observed among other things,—

Apud Assyrios Bel dicitur, quādam sacrorum ratione, et Saturnus et Sol;—
Among the Assyrians, by some system of sacred matters, both Saturn and Sol are called Bel.

MOVERS regards this as the first proof of the fact in question, and he gives no others which prove any more.

54. But who will assume on the ground of this that eight centuries earlier the planet Saturn was worshipped under the name of Baal? Nothing is said here about a *planet*; and

though it is very possible that the Asiatic astrologers, shortly before or after the beginning of our Epoch, gave the name 'Star of Baal' to the planet which the Greeks called 'Star of Kronos,' (for which, however, I can find no proof,) others have connected the 'Star of Baal' with Jupiter. (See SANCH. *ed.* ORELL. *p.*43, where a passage is quoted from JABLONSKY, *Panth. Ægypt.*)

55. Who then is Baal? The Sun? MOVERS maintains this also,* and produces more proofs for this than for the combination with Kronos, though all out of a time many centuries later than Solomon. I believe that the question, as to what astrological meaning lies at the foundation of Baal-worship, cannot be answered; since, as far back as we can reckon, astrology either did not exist at all in Western Asia before the time of the Assyrians or Chaldæans, or, at all events, exercised no influence upon religion.⁵⁵

56. Appeal is made for the contrary to MOVERS; and there is some wisdom in this,—since out of his work may be proved whatever one wishes to prove. On this point he is altogether at variance with himself. He allows, *p.*67, that the influence of astrology entered the religions of Western Asia only subsequently to the Assyrian times,—that it came, not from Egypt, but from Chaldæa, *p.*316,—that, in any case, an influence might be assumed of Phœnicia upon Egypt, rather than the contrary, *p.*39,40,—that the old Phœnician religion had no astrological foundation whatever, *p.*316,—that for this there was need also of a priestly caste, which should apply itself to astronomy, and bring it into connection with religion,—but that in any case a simple worship preceded it, *p.*167.

⁵⁵ But, surely, it did not need 'astrological' Science to fix attention on the *Sun*, as the Great (apparent) Lord (Baal) of Nature. The question about *Saturn* is very much more obscure. The Sun must have been regarded as 'the Baal' in very early pre-scientific times.

---

* I.*p.*180-185; elsewhere Baal is combined with Mars, *p.*187,188; sometimes Baal (Herakles) is named a son of Saturn, *p.*267.—OORT.

57. But, on the other hand, he asserts that the Phœnician Deities had already, before the time of the Chaldæans, a 'sidereal meaning,' *p.*65,—that Mosaism was an advance upon the Saturn-worship of Western Asia, *p.*315,—that—

the planet Saturn was already in earlier times the Supreme God of Semitism, as is shown, at all events, by the institution of the Sabbath, by Moses hallowing the number 'seven,' by Saturn being regarded as the father of Jupiter and the other gods in Greece and Italy. *p.*313.

He produces no proof for all this.[57]

58. Up to this time, as far as I am aware, no evidences have been brought forward to show the astrological signification of the Asiatic Divine Names. And if, in respect of our knowledge of the ancient religions, we desire to stand in some sense on firm ground, we must be humble, and not say that we know more than our sources of information supply to us. Nothing whatever is known of an astrological meaning of Baal. We know nothing of what happened in primeval times in the heart of Asia.[58]

59. The O.T. gives us the oldest notions about the worship of Baalim. And this is certain that under the name 'Baal' the Israelites understood neither the Sun nor the Moon nor the Planets. At all events, together with Beth-Shemesh (House of the Sun) we find mention made of Kirjath-Baal (City of Baal); and, when the Assyrians brought the Star-worship into Israel, Baal was distinguished from the Sun, Moon, and Planets, 2K.xxi.3,5,xxiii.5.*[59]

[57] We agree entirely with Dr. Oort in rejecting the notion of an *astrological* origin of the early religion of the Phœnicians and Hebrews,—of its having any relation to the planet Saturn, which was probably not discovered till a much later age. But the worship of the Sun and Moon is, surely, most *natural*, and is not to be called astrological.

[58] We do not need to be told that in primitive times the Sun *must* have been worshipped under some name or other. And what name more likely than 'the Baal' = 'the Lord,' *i.e.* the Lord of all Creation?

[59] The mention of 'Beth-Shemesh' in close connection with 'Kirjath-Baal'

---

* Movers mentions also a Palmyrene inscription, בעל שמש.—Oort.

60. Or is, perhaps, the hallowing of the Sabbath, and generally of the number 'seven,' supposed to prove that the original worship of Israel rests on an astrological basis? This is maintained by MOVERS, and, treading in his steps, by Prof. DOZY, *p.*38, and many others. But on what ground? That later Rabbins named Saturn 'Sabbethai,' proves surely nothing. When once the last day of the week was called 'Saturn's Day,' the naming of the planet was very natural. That Jews of the fifteenth century after Christ called Saturn the 'Star of Israel,' is easily to be explained by their knowledge of the passage in SANCHONIATHON, *ed.* ORELL. *p.*42, about which more presently. That at a certain time the Sabbath, instead of the *last*, became the *first* day of the week, has been maintained indeed by MOVERS, *p.*38, and Prof. DOZY, but not established by any proof.

seems rather to show that the Sun *was* the object of worship by the Canaanite tribes under the name of 'the Baal,' and this is further confirmed by the Palmyrene inscription, quoted by MOVERS, בעל שמש, *Baal Shemesh*, = 'Lord Sun.' It is plain from the name Beth-Shemesh that the Sun was worshipped in Canaan: and if so, would he not most naturally have been called 'the Baal'?

From the fact that the worship of 'the Baal' is distinguished in later days from the astrological worship of the Sun, Moon, and Planets, introduced by the Assyrians, we may infer two things:—

(i) That the Hebrew worship before the Assyrian time—including that of the Canaanitish tribes from which it was adopted, and therefore including also the worship of the Sun as at Beth-Shemesh,—was *natural*, and not astrological;

(ii) That, at the time when the Hebrews adopted the worship of the Syro-Phœnician tribes of Canaan, the development of that worship had already made some progress, so that the original meaning of the worship, as addressed to the *Sun*, had already been lost sight of to a great extent, at any rate by the multitude; and thus the Hebrews adopted merely the *externals* of their worship, without realising the inner significance of it.

Just so, in Roman-Catholic countries, the people, probably, in many cases, actually worship the images and pictures themselves, while to higher minds they are only symbols of the hidden objects of worship. And probably another ruder race, learning religion from them, but only half-instructed, like the Indians of Chili, would be still less able to look through the signs to the things signified.

In this way we may, perhaps, account for the fact that the old natural worship of 'the Baal'—the meaning of which, as actually Sun-worship, had almost been lost,—was distinguished from the new astrological worship of the 'Sun, Moon, and Planets,' introduced by the Assyrians.

61. But, if the institution of the Sabbath, and the hallowing of the number 'seven,' are not to be explained from astrological calculations, it may be asked, From what, then, were they derived? I do not know. The oldest injunction for the sanctifying of the Sabbath says only—

'that thine ox and thine ass may rest, and that the son of thy maid and the stranger may draw breath.' E.xxiii.12.

No *religious* reason (in the strict sense of the word) is given for it: and thus the ancient Israelites seem to have found in it nothing but a humane command. It was only in later times that it came to be regarded as a sign of the covenant, or as a consequence of the rest of God after the work of Creation.[60]

62. Why may not the division of the month into four equal portions be the ground of it,—although they do not come out with an exact number of days, and although the New Moon did not always fall on the Sabbath? If we will not be content with a *non liquet*, this hypothesis is at all events more natural than that on this account alone we should assume an astrological basis for the worship of Israel. Let us just consider the consequences which would follow necessarily from such an assumption.

63 There must have existed first an artless, simple, kind of worship; for, of course, human beings did not begin by praying to the Sun, Moon, and five Planets, of which Saturn was the highest because his orbit was the highest. Then a priestly caste must have come into existence, who would occupy themselves with astronomy, and build up an artificial religious system upon their observations. Let us assume that this took place; and so the day of the Planet Baal (Saturn) became the first of the seven, and Baal the chief Deity. All this must have happened in the heart of Asia, *e.g.* in Ur of the Chaldees,

---

[60] The Elohist, however, writing in a very early time, has clearly meant, in G.ii.1-3, to commend the observance of the Sabbath as a day of *rest*, (he says nothing about *worship*,) on the ground of God's resting from the work of Creation.

long before the time when the Canaanitish tribes, and among them the Hebrews, left those regions.

64. These, however, had lost all knowledge of this astrological meaning; and so the Hebrews, by order of Moses, hallowed not the *first*, but the *last*, day of the week; and, whether the other tribes had retained any idea of it, is unknown. So far also as we know, the Israelites never named the days of the week with the names of gods. Nor can it be shown that anything of this kind was done in Egypt. At all events, the oldest trace of it appears in HERODOTUS, ii.82,—that is, in the fifth century before Christ, long after the Chaldee influence had extended itself thither. In Israel and the surrounding tribes, Baal was a general name for the Deity, while the duties connected with the honouring of some Baals *point most to Sun-worship* [N.B.], of which more presently.

65. Then in the eighth century B.C., through Assyrian influences, Star-worship was introduced into Israel and elsewhere. 'Baal' comes now into connection with 'Sun, Moon, and Planets,'—but as if they had never had any previous acquaintance with each other. The Assyrians, also, and Chaldæans seem to have known nothing of any such a relationship, and hence seem never to have named subsequently any Planet with the name 'Baal.' Some centuries later, the Greek Divine Names make their entrance into Phœnicia and Syria: Venus is combined with Astarte, Moloch with Mars, Baal or Bel with Jupiter, sometimes also with Saturn. Astrology names the Planets with the Divine Names; and so Baal gets his old meaning [of 'Saturn'] again.

66. This most extraordinary course of development must be assumed, if an astrological basis is to be assigned to the worship of Baal. Briefly, this is how we should have to state the history of this religion: First, simple worship,—then an astrological system,—again simple worship of Baal, in which all priestly lore was forgotten,—lastly, once more astrology. All this must

be assumed without any proof, merely because the hallowing of the number 'seven' cannot be explained otherwise.[61]

67. One word more,—and we dismiss our 'Baal-Saturn' once for all. Professor Dozy produces, in support of his view that Saturn was the God of Israel, a passage from SANCHONIA-THON, *p*.42, *ed.* ORELL., where Saturn, according to him, bears the surname 'Israel.' If we look well at this passage, and take into account the character of Philo, from whose pen the words have come, we shall see that it allows of another and a much more probable explanation. He says that it was customary in the olden time, in great dangers, to sacrifice children, and that Kronos, an ancient king, after whose name the Planet was called, in order to avert disaster in a war, sacrificed his only-begotten son by the nymph *Anobreth* (עֵין עִבְרִית = *Eyn-ibrith*, 'Hebrew fountain'),—appending to the name Kronos the remark, 'whom the Phœnicians name *Israel.*'

68. What follows from this? Just this—that Philo, wishing to explain euhemeristically* the myth of the child-devouring Kronos, combines with it a Jewish-Phœnician legend about a *king*, 'Israel,' who sacrificed his only-begotten *Jeud* (יחיד, *comp.* G.xxii.2,12,16'. If Israel had been the name of a *Deity*, he would not have gained his point with this. Probably, he

---

[61] To the remarks of Dr. OORT in (60–66) we, for the most part, entirely assent —only repeating that the worship of the *Sun*, as 'the Baal,' did not (as we suppose) spring from *astrological* science, but from the most natural causes, such as produce among the Aryan race in Western India the conceptions, whence the mythology of Greece is now known to have originated—causes quite as natural, as those which in Dr. OORT's view, as in ours, may have led even in very early times to the definition of the week as the approximate fourth part of a lunation, during which the Moon passes from one of her four principal phases to another. The words, which we have italicised at the end of (64), tend to confirm our view that the Sun was 'the Baal' in the primitive worship of the tribes of Canaan.

---

* After the example of EUHEMERUS, who sought to explain the *myths* of the old religion as arising from *legends* about ancient heroes, &c. who actually lived in the olden time. *Ed.*

is referring here to Abraham's sacrifice. Among the Damascenes also, in the old legend, Abraham appears as king, together with Israel. MOVERS,i.*p.*87.

69. What kind of a Deity, then, was Baal? In Babylon, in Phœnicia and its colonies, and in the surrounding peoples, who were branches out of the same stem, Israelites, Moabites, Ammonites, Philistines, Amorites, &c. we find a Divine Name 'Baal.' Whether the children of Israel brought it with them into Canaan, or adopted it there from the old inhabitants, cannot be determined with certainty, since we have neither literature of the Mosaic time, nor many [? any] genuine historical names of that age or older. Most probably, they brought it with them.

70. About this 'Baal,' however, two different views are held. Some regard it as a general Divine Name, of like meaning with El or Elohim. Others, among whom is MOVERS, assume a separate Deity of this Name, of which different modifications are presented to us in the O.T. It is not possible to arrive at certainty in this matter. In respect of this, however, the same remark holds good, which I made before, when discussing the question whether the religions of Western Asia had an astrological basis, *viz.* that we must not assume more than we know.

71. Whether in very ancient times there existed a unity of religion among the Semitic tribes, in which a Deity was worshipped under the name of Baal, distinguished from other Gods, is quite unknown. The name 'Baal,'=Lord, points to a general idea, as El, Elohim, Adonis, Moloch, Jupiter, Zeus, &c. And from the manner in which this name is used in the O.T. we may see that, in the first centuries of the existence of Israel as a people, no particular Deity was understood by it.

72. (i) Thus, first, with the name 'Baal' was coupled the name of the tribe or race, in which a Sanctuary stood, *e.g.* the

Baal of Judah, of Gad, &c. So among other peoples we find the Baal of Tyre, of Libya, &c. Mov.i.p.175.

(ii) In inscriptions, also, it is coupled with a pronoun, as Baalan, ' our Baal.' Ib.p.172.

(iii) Further, more precise descriptions are added, in order to define the worship connected with a Baal, as 'Baal-Berith' = Baal of the Covenant, 'Baal-Zebub' = Baal of flies, 'Baal-Shemesh' = Baal of the Sun,* 'Baal-Samin' = Baal of the Heavens, &c. Ib.p.174.

(iv) Divine Names also are added to it, as Baal-Chiun (Chivan), Baal-Moloch. Ib.p.173,174.

(v) Lastly, the word was often used by the Hebrews in the plural and with the article, when a special anti-JHVH-istic worship made its way into the land (about which presently).

73. All these phenomena are to be explained very easily, if we assume that they understood nothing more by the word 'Baal' than by 'El,'—but with great difficulty, if we find in it the name of one distinct Deity. The inscription, 'To our lord Melkarth [מֶלֶךְ קֶרֶת, *melech kereth*, ' king of the city,'] Baal of Tyre,' Mov.p.178, is strongly against this. 'Baal-Berith' again is connected with 'El-Berith,' Ju.ix.46. As it seems to me, SERVIUS speaks not improbably the truth when he says, †—

Unde et linguâ Punicâ Bel Deus dicitur,
Whence also in the Phœnician tongue God is called Bel.

---

* Should not 'Baal-Shemesh' rather fall into the next category, together with Baal-Moloch, &c.? And it may be possible that the name 'Baal-Berith' may have some connection with the 'goddess of Lebanon,' mentioned by MOVERS, i.p.575,&c., 'whom SANCHONIATHON names with the Phœnician name Βηρούθ,' this name being derived from the Phœnician and Aramaic ברות, Heb. ברוש, meaning 'cypress,' the symbol of the goddess being probably an Ashera of cypresswood ?—*Ed.*

† MOVERS,i.p.285. Another quotation, which tends to show that Baal was still in later times a general name for 'God,' is to be found on p.187, from *Chron. Pasch.* &c.—Ἕως τῆς νῦν καλοῦσι περσιστὶ τὸν Βάαλ θεόν, &c., 'Up to the present time they (the Assyrians) call God in the Persian tongue *the Baal*,'—and Βάαλ περσιστὶ λέγεται θεὸς ὅς ἐστιν ὁ πολεμικὸς Ἄρης, 'in Persian Baal is the name of the God who is the warlike Ares.'—OORT.

74. Might not then JHVH be called the Baal of Israel? Most certainly; and that this was really the case Hosea shows when he says, ii.16,—

'And this shall happen in that day, saith JHVH, that thou shalt call me Ishi (my husband) and shalt call me no more Baali (my lord).'

The same is testified by the Proper Name Baaljah (בעליה, [='Jah is Baal'] LXX, Βααλιά).

75. That anciently, however, the name 'Baal' had absolutely nothing anti-JHVH-istic in it, is shown plainly from 2S.v.20, where we read,—

'Then came David to Baal-Perazim, and slew them (the Philistines) there, and said, 'JHVH has burst (פָּרַץ) mine enemies before my face, as a burst of water': therefore one called the name of the place Baal-Perazim.'

The derivation is strange enough, and the true meaning will probably be 'Baal of Perazim,' [where 'Perazim' denotes the family of Perez,] the greatest family of Judah,—just as in Is.xxviii.21 we find mentioned a 'mount of Perazim.' But the etymology is remarkable, inasmuch as the inventor of it, who must have lived after David, saw no difficulty in the name 'Baal,' and translated it by JHVH—[that is, he derived the name 'Baal-Perazim' from the fact that 'JHVH had burst (*paraz*) &c.']⁶²

---

⁶² 'Baal-Perazim' means most probably, as Dr. OORT says, 'Baal of Perazim,'—*i.e.* it was a place belonging to the family of Perez, where there was a Sanctuary of the Baal. The later writer—whether living in or after David's time—had manifestly no such a horror of the name 'Baal,' as a still later writer, *e.g.* of the time of Josiah, would have had; and the phenomenon, which we have here before us, is precisely similar to that which occurs with the Jehovistic writer in G.xvi.11, where we read 'Thou shalt call his name Ishma-El (=*El* hears), for *Jehovah* hath heard thy affliction,'—the two names 'El' and 'Jehovah' being here treated as interchangeable, just as 'Baal' and 'Jehovah' are in 2S.v.20. In fact, the names Eshbaal, Meribbaal, and Baalyadah, of the sons of Saul, Jonathan, and David, imply distinctly that in David's time no such feeling existed,—that JEHOVAH might be called by good men 'the Baal' of Israel, as JHVH was by the multitude.

Yet it is remarkable that in not one passage of the Psalms is 'Baal' used with reference to JHVH, nor in any passage of the Prophets, except the verse of Hosea, ii.16, quoted in (74). This seems rather to imply, as we have said (note ⁵⁵) that the more advanced and spiritually-minded Psalmists and Prophets did not

76. *Before the time of Ahab there existed no anti-JHVH-istic worship of Baal in Israel.*

This proposition seems to be contradicted by the testimonies of Ju.ii.11,13, iii.7, vi.10,25 ; *comp.* also x.6,13, 1S.vii.4, xii.10, where we read continually,—

'They forsook JHVH and served the Baalim and Ashtaroth (Astartes).'

But these notices are not trustworthy. They come from the hand of the Compiler (or Compilers), who regarded the history from his own point of view, and, not being able to conceive of any public calamity without a previous apostasy from JHVH, ascribes the defeats of the people to idolatry. He had no correct idea of the ancient time, as appears at once from the general mention of Baals and Astartes, whose worship was, perhaps, closely combined in his days. He attaches manifestly no distinct idea to these names, but employs them for any idols whatsoever.[63]

77. Generally, the Jews understood little of the ancient state of things. For instance, Jeroboam's calf-worship itself was regarded by the Chronicler as idolatry, 2Ch.xiii.8,9 ;[64] and all

---

like to use the name 'Baal' in connection with JEHOVAH; though doubtless the people used it freely in connection with JHVH, and Saul, Jonathan, and even David could give their sons names compounded with 'Baal.'

[63] This agrees with our own view, as stated in note [49], that at the time when the Israelites entered Canaan, and took over the worship of 'the Baal' from the Canaanites, the true meaning of this worship, as addressed originally to the Sun, had faded away even among the Canaanites themselves, and must therefore have existed very faintly—if at all—among the Israelites even of that day, and very soon disappeared among them altogether. Hence in Josiah's time the worship of 'the Baal' was a mere unmeaning idolatry, and is mentioned separately from that of the 'Sun, Moon, and Planets,' 2K.xxiii.5.

[64] This, of course, is said by Dr. OORT on the supposition that the objection felt to Jeroboam's doings in matters of religion was *originally* not at all that he had *set up calves*, but that he had set them up in *Dan* and *Bethel*, and called the people to worship *there* instead of at Jerusalem. This is very probably true, as regards the objections felt on this subject by the mass of the *people* of Judah : but it may be doubted if it applies to the Prophets and men of higher mind among them, who probably condemned even in that age the worship of the *calves*—in other words, the worship of JHVH instead of JEHOVAH—as idolatry. At all events, no proof has

image-worship was held by the Jews to be such, *comp.* the close combination of the First and Second Commandments in the edition of the Decalogue in E.xx.3–6.[65] A remarkable example of the confused ideas of the Compiler of our historical Books is the misuse of the name Ashera [E.V. 'grove']. This word expressed originally a pillar on or near—not only the altars of Baal, but also—the altars of JHVH—E.xxxiv. 13, D.vii.5,xii.3,xvi.21, Ju.vi.25,26,28,30, 1K.xiv.15,23,2K.xiii.6, xvii.10,16,xviii.4,xxi.3,xxiii.15, 2Ch.xiv.3,xvii.6,xxxi.1,xxxiii.3, 19,xxxiv.3,4,7, Is.xvii.8, Jer.xvii.2, Mic.v.13. The word means this also in 2Ch.xv.16 and 1K.xv.13; for we must there translate,—

'She (Asa's mother) made on the Ashera something detestable (מִפְלֶצֶת).'

What the 'detestable' thing was, is not explained; but it was probably the αἰδοῖα γυναῖκος, which HERODOTUS saw on similar pillars, ii.106.[66]—['I myself saw them in Syria of Palestine.']

been adduced to show the contrary; and in 1K.xii.28–31 much the same language is used about Jeroboam's calves—doubtless, by a writer of a much later age, but still, probably, living before the Captivity—as is employed by the Chronicler.

[65] The Decalogue (*App.*I) was written, as we believe, about the age of Josiah. *Before* that time, we may gather that image-worship was not altogether forbidden in Judah, even in the reigns of pious kings; *e.g.* the Brazen Serpent was worshipped till the days of Hezekiah, 2K.xviii.4; and plainly Josiah had allowed image-worship to be practised for the first seventeen years of his reign, 2K.xxiii.4,6,14.

[66] It seems plain that the Ashera (from אָשַׁר, *ashar*, 'be straight, erect') was in reality a phallus, like the *Linga* or *Lingam* of the Hindoos, the sign of the male organ of generation, employed as the symbol of the energising, life-giving, power of the Sun. It was exhibited in various forms—sometimes, in rude representations of the actual object, but usually in a more refined form, as a trunk of a tree, dead or living, a *pillar*, &c.: *comp.* the 'round towers' of Ireland, which are supposed by some to belong to the Sun-worship. In India, a compound form is habitually used, the *Linga* and *Yoni*, exhibiting in symbols, for the most part artistically disguised, both the male and female organs. Such 'Lingas' are found all over India, Japan, &c. The fact, that Asa's mother had the 'detestable' thing expressed in some way on one of these erections, shows plainly the nature of the Ashera itself.

So writes MOVERS, i.*p.*571:—

'In the O.T. we have one passage referring to the idol Ashera, which leaves no just doubt that it was a *phallus*. The annalist of the history of the Kings speaks of the worship of the Ashera introduced by Rehoboam, and of the Sodomites con-

78. In 2K.xxi.7, xxiii.6, Ashera appears as the name of a goddess: but the oldest reading is to be found in 2Ch.xxxiii.7, 15, where סֶמֶל (? image) stands instead of אֲשֵׁרָה: the alteration is probably due to the Compiler of Kings.* Ashera stands as the name of a goddess in Ju.iii.7, in place of Astarte, which is usual elsewhere, and in 1K.xviii.19, in the legend of Elijah, where her prophets are merely mentioned at the beginning, in order to disappear thenceforward without a trace: this record, consequently, is anything but old and authentic: [but see note [17]].

79. It cannot be shown that under Ahab a worship of Astarte was introduced together with the worship of Baal.[67] Nor can it be made out certainly when Ashera became a goddess of like meaning with Astarte. We must therefore help ourselves with a conjecture. In front of the Temple of Baal in Samaria stood an Ashera, which long survived the Temple itself, 1K.xvi.31,32, 2K.x.18-27,xiii.6. Perhaps, when Assyrians and Israelites were mixed in the northern kingdom, this was honoured as a goddess or as a symbol of Astarte. By the Jews, who naturally did not understand much of this worship, it was identified with Astarte, and by our Compiler [? in Ju.iii.7, 1K.xviii.19,] reproduced in the detestable Asheras of the olden time.[68]

nected with it, 1K.xiv.23,24; and he adds that the Queen-Mother Maachah made a figure-of-shame on the Ashera, which Asa *hewed-down* and burnt in the valley of Kidron, 1K.xv.13, 2Ch.xv.16. What is here translated literally 'figure-of-shame' is in Hebrew מִפְלֶצֶת, *i.e.* properly, *pudendum, verendum*, as also JEROME explains it, who translates the passage of Chronicles thus: *Sed et Maacham matrem Asa regis ex augusto deposuit imperio, eò quod fecisset in luco* (לַאֲשֵׁרָה) *simulacrum Priapi: comp.* JER. *Comm.* ad Hos.iv. From the comparison of this passage according to which the wooden idol Ashera was a *pudendum*, with the other which indicates it as a high pillar, it is plain that it was a *phallus*, a symbol of the generating and fructifying power of nature.'

[67] That is, together with the worship of the *Tyrian* Baal, of which Dr. OORT is going to speak presently.

[68] Probably, in the later times of Judah, when the Assyrian 'astrological' worship of the Sun, Moon, and Planets, had altogether obliterated the notion, that

---

* In 2K.xxiii.7 the reading is indistinct and uncertain: the LXX has χεττιίμ. OORT.

80. After this digression, we return again to the Baalim. The notices of an anti-JHVH-istic Baal-worship in Judges and Samuel are untrustworthy. Solomon had established various worships by his royal authority, that of Astarte, Milcom, and Chemosh, but not of Baal. An *idol* Baal did not exist in Israel before the time of Ahab.[69]

81. As far as we can make out from the passages where the Baalim are mentioned, either they were subordinate deities subject to JHVH, the honouring of whom did not, in the estimation of the people, detract from the worship of the God of Israel, or else, in the Sanctuaries named 'Baal of Judah,' 'Baal of the Well,' &c., originally none but JHVH was worshipped.[70] We must not in any case seek for pure Monotheism in ancient Israel,[71]—much less, apostasy from JHVH. Even in Jeremiah's days, the people still maintained that they were not defiled, that they had not followed after the Baalim, Jer.ii.23; though the Prophet objected to them that they had built as many altars for the Baal, as there were streets in Jerusalem, xi.13. See N.B. at the end of this Section, *p*.63.

82. The Baalim—if under this name were understood deities distinct from JHVH, and if any account was taken of their relation to the God of Israel,—were equivalent to *mediators*

---

the original Baal-worship in Israel had reference to the Sun, (notes [59], [68]), the Ashera too may have lost all significance as a symbol of Sun-worship, and may have come, like the Baal himself, 2K.xxiii.5, to be treated as a separate idol.

[69] That is to say, before Ahab's time, the '*Syrian* Baal,' JHVH, was worshipped in Israel as 'the Baal': but Ahab introduced the worship of the '*Tyrian* Baal,' and that was regarded as 'idolatrous.'

[70] This entirely agrees with our view, that *everywhere* in Canaan, before and after the arrival of the Israelites, the same Deity, *viz.* the Sun, was worshipped as 'the Baal,' whose great mysterious name was JHVH. In other words the different 'Baalim' all represented 'the Baal,' JHVH, as the different 'Virgins' throughout the world—'our Lady of Loretto,' 'our Lady of Salette,' &c.—all represent 'our Lady,' the Virgin Mary.

[71] Except, perhaps, among a few great minds, as Samuel, &c. But even these regarded Jehovah rather as the *Supreme* Deity, the 'God of Gods,' than as the *only* God, which idea is first clearly expressed by the Deuteronomist, iv.35,39,vi.4, xxxii.39; see *P*.III.546.iii.

between JHVH and the people. Hence is to be explained 1S.ii.25,—

'If a man sin against a man, then will the Elohim intercede for him: but, if a man sin against JHVH, who then shall pray for him?'[72]

The oldest legislation seems to recognise and to legalise these 'Elohim,' forbidding to curse them, E.xxii.28, (*comp.* xxi.6, xxii.8,9)—*v.*20 is introduced awkwardly,[73]—and it understands by them nothing anti-JHVH-istic, since in the Sanctuaries, where difficult questions were determined by the Divine judgment, the oath was taken in the name of JHVH, *v.*11.[74] JHVH was the God of Gods, and next to him the 'Baalim' or 'Elohim' were honoured.[75]

83. In saying this, I do not wish to assert that *all* the Deities bore this name, and that 'Baalim' is convertible with 'Elohim.'

---

[72] I cannot assent to Dr.Oort's view of this passage. It seems to me that in 1S.ii.25 as well as in E.xxi.6, xxii.8,9, xxii.28, 'Elohim' must be used of the 'mighty-ones,' the 'authorities,' the 'powers that be'; especially as in E.xxii.28 the command, 'thou shalt not revile the Elohim,' stands in a parallelism with 'neither shalt thou curse the ruler of thy people.' See Geiger, *p.*272. There may be a reference also to the fact that the 'authorities' decided difficult cases, which were brought before them for judgment, *in the Sanctuary*, in the presence of or by the help of the Divine Power (הָאֱלֹהִים): *comp.*Ju.xx.1,18,23,26–28, xxi.2,3, 1S.xxii.15, &c.

[73] With the view just enunciated in note [72], there is no 'awkwardness' whatever in *v.*20.

[74] The fact, that all oaths were taken in the name of JHVH, tends also to confirm our view of the case,—*viz.* that the 'Baalim' everywhere represented JHVH.

[75] I see no reason for supposing that '*next* to JHVH the Baalim were honoured.' JHVH *was* 'the Baal'—was Elohim—was the Elohim. But in later days, as Solomon's, *other* Deities, besides JHVH, had been introduced—'strange Gods,' 'foreign Elohim,'—as Milcom, Chemosh, Astarte, and these were forbidden; perhaps, because upon the basis of such names as these the Prophets could not hope to build up a purer faith, and establish the purer worship of Jehovah, the Living God, as they could, and eventually did, upon the basis of the name JHVH.

So, as we have said, among the Zulus in the present day, Missionaries would be content—rather would desire and endeavour—to retain the native name for the Deity, Unkulunkulu, 'Great-Great-One,' as being very well fitted to express the Divine Being. We should not condemn as idolatrous the mere fact of their worshipping Unkulunkulu, however unbecoming and incongruous their ceremonies might be; we should only strive to elevate their ideas, and purify their *mode* of worshipping. But we should object to the use of any *unsuitable* name of their own, or any *outlandish* name of some foreign Deity.

But neither will I say the contrary. Whether they are distinguished in Jer.xi.13, or not, is not plain. If they are, there must then have been Gods (Elohim), who did not bear the name of Baalim; and, since the worshipping of trees and stones points to tree- and stone-deities, and also Satyrs were probably worshipped (see 111,112), these are, perhaps, to be distinguished from the Baalim.[76] Here, however, we are groping altogether in the dark. The Elohim were for the Israelites what the Saints and 'Our dear Lady' of this or that place are for Roman-Catholics. The honouring of these does not in the view of the worshippers derogate at all from the worship paid to the One God, although, perhaps, they appeal most to the subordinate deities.[77]

84. The Israelites of later days—[Dr. OORT means 'the days of Samuel and David,' not the still later days of Josiah]—had no such great reason, therefore, to be afraid of the use of the name Baal. It is an anachronism to understand under that name, in the days of Samuel and David, a Deity which entrapped away the honour of the national God, JHVH. It was only in later days, after Ahab's time, that he became this.[78]

[76] The 'trees' and 'stones' seem to have been only different forms of the phallus or Linga (note ⁑), and, as such, they were representatives of the one Baal, the Sun, who appears under different names as the Baal of this place or that.

[77] Dr. OORT's comparison is not exactly correct. The state of things in Israel, according to our view, may be compared more properly with the worship of the one Virgin, of whom there are various representatives, as 'our Lady of' this place or that, than with that of the numerous Saints, who are for the most part different patrons of different places. But the Virgin, though deemed almost all-powerful as a mediator, is yet subordinated to the Supreme Being; whereas with the Israelites 'Elohim' or 'the ELOHIM' was only another name for the Supreme Being Himself,—the Baal of Israel, JHVH, (or in the minds of pious worshippers, JEHOVAH); it was not a mere synonym for 'the Baalim.'

[78] Though before the time of Ahab, who introduced the worship of the Tyrian Baal, the Prophets do not seem to have openly *condemned* the use of the name 'Baal' as applied to JHVH, yet they evidently, as we have said, did not affect the use of it, for it appears nowhere in any Psalm or Prophecy, applied to JHVH, except in Hos.ii.16: and so in *v.*17 the Prophet goes on to say, 'For I will take away the names of the Baalim out of her mouth, and they shall no more be remembered by their name.'

85. With this view of the Baalim, the story of Gideon or Jerubbaal seems to be irreconcilable. Yet we are very far from possessing this story in an unmutilated form. Gideon's surname, Jerubbaal, cannot, in my judgment, mean anything else than 'Baal-defender.' That this name for a 'defender of JHVH' offended pious men of later times, is not to be wondered at. They have devised two modes of removing this stumbling-block out of the way. The first was the very usual mode of changing Jerub*baal* into Jerub*besheth*, 2S.xi.21, wherein they seem to have overlooked 1S.xii.11. The other was to give a Jehovistic etymology to the name; and with this view the account in Ju.vi.25–32 was excogitated, and Jerubbaal accordingly was explained to mean, 'one with whom Baal strives.'

86. The Compiler of the account in the Judges has done his best to erase every trace of a friendly relation between Gideon and the Baal-Berith = ' Baal of the Covenant' at Shechem; and accordingly he mentions, viii.33–35, that it was not till after Gideon's death that the Baalim were served, and Baal-Berith in particular. But ix.2 reveals the truth to us, where we read that Abimelech after Gideon's death put the question to the Shechemites,—

'Which is best, that seventy men, all sons of Jerubbaal, should reign over you, or that one man should be prince over you?'

This dilemma would not have been stated thus, if Jerubbaal had not himself ruled previously over them,—if not as King, yet as Judge. When Abimelech thus laid claim to the Sovereignty, the Temple of Baal-Berith was already at Shechem, *v.*4. The worship of Baal-Berith, or El-Berith, ix.46, then, [was practised under Gideon's rule, and, consequently,] was not anti-JHVH-istic. Gideon, the valiant 'defender of JHVH,' certainly took part in it with a clear conscience, and bore the name of 'Baal-defender.'[79]

[79] I cannot wholly agree with Dr. Oort's views as to the story of Gideon. It appears to me that the name 'Jerubbaal' cannot well denote 'he strives for Baal' = Baal-defender, as I understand Dr. Oort to explain the word; but, after the analogy

87. Now, however, we must examine into the reasons which caused this great change in the conception of the Baalim. How did Baal become an idolatrous name in Israel? Two circumstances contributed to this, *the inner development of JHVH-ism*, and *the threatening form, which the worship of the Tyrian Baal assumed under Ahab*. A word on both these points.

88. From the days of Moses, Israel was the people of JHVH. He was no true Israelite, who left the altars of JHVH unvisited and sware not by JHVH.[80] But what kind of JHVH-ism was

of Ishmael = 'El hears,' Ishmaiah = 'Jah hears,' &c., so Jerubbaal must denote 'Baal strives,' as the Scripture story explains it. But the analogy of these other names makes it most unlikely that Gideon was called Jerubbaal, in order to imply hostility between him and the Baal, as if the Baal had striven or would strive with *him*. The Divine Name, El or Jah, is always (as far as I am aware) meant to *honour* the person in whose name it appears, and to extend a kind of protection to him: and the compound name usually expresses some general attribute or quality of the Deity, 'El hears,' 'Jah hears,' &c., as it seems to do here, 'Baal strives.' This name, then, given to Gideon, seems to show that he was under the protection of the Baal, and therefore was his servant. And this is confirmed by the fact, to which Dr. OORT refers, that in Shechem, under Gideon's government, there was a Temple of Baal-Berith or El-Berith, Ju.ix.4,46—upon which see (72*)—and also by the circumstance recorded in viii.27, that 'Gideon made an ephod, and put it in his city, in Ophrah; and all Israel went thither a whoring after it; which thing became a snare unto Gideon and to his house.' This does not look as if Gideon was such a strenuous opponent of all idolatry.

How then are the contradictions of the story to be explained? I cannot think that Dr. OORT is right in regarding vi.25-32 as an interpolation: it seems to me to be a portion of the context in which it appears. Nevertheless, it is plain that two hands, at least, have been concerned in the composition of this story as it now stands, for the reasons stated at length in *App*.IV: and this fact may explain the discrepancies.

[80] We agree *generally* with Dr. OORT's account of 'the inner development of JHVH-ism' in (87-96); but there are some points in respect of which our view, it will be seen, differs somewhat from his. Thus we see no ground for believing that Israel 'from the days of Moses was the people of JHVH.' On the contrary, in *P*.V.Chap.xix, we have given reasons for believing that, though Israel may have known the name JHVH very soon after their entrance into Canaan, (that is, very nearly from the time of the Exodus = the 'days of Moses,') yet JHVH was not distinctly recognised as the 'God of Israel,' and Israel did not formally regard itself as the 'people of JHVH,' till the time of Samuel. In short, Dr. OORT, while admitting the unhistorical character of all the main details of the Pentateuchal story,—as the revelation of the Divine Name to Moses, the construction of the Tabernacle, &c.— yet assumes it to be true, without (as it seems to me) any sufficient reason (see note[48]), that Moses did actually teach the people the worship of JHVH, the Deity worshipped in his tribe or family (on which see note [84]).

this? If Ezra and his companions had been able to cast a single glance upon the religious condition of the people of the time of the Judges and long afterwards, what strange things would they have seen! They would, perhaps, have understood what a folly they were committing in placing at the head of the history the Legislation contained in Exodus-Deuteronomy.

89. The whole religious life of the Israelites was a fearful contrast with the Law. Upon every hill, and under every green tree, altars were erected, on which and by which were placed pillars (Asheras) and sun-images (Chammanim). Memorial-stones were to be found everywhere, sprinkled with oil, and honoured with sacrifices. Countless deities were worshipped as private gods and mediators with JHVH.[81] Rude and arbitrary was the worship. Priests of the tribe of Levi might minister at Shiloh and other renowned Sanctuaries;[82] any one who chose sacrificed besides wherever he pleased. Invocation of the holy flame and the altar-incense were coupled with processions round the altars.[83]

90. At the Sanctuaries, in which frequently images of JHVH were placed, festivals were celebrated and sacrificial feasts observed, the chief characteristic of which was 'making merry before the face of JHVH.' There women served as well as men: there were the sacred dances conducted: there the Priest, according to his right, had his portion of the flesh of the sacrifice dragged out of the cauldron, and claimed sometimes (to the disgust of the worshippers) what was not yet cooked.

---

[81] I have said already (note [75]) why I doubt the correctness of this statement that the numerous Baalim were 'private gods and mediators with JHVH.' They were no more so than the numerous Virgins in different chapels throughout the Roman-Catholic world are 'private' objects of worship, and 'mediators with Mary.'

[82] The 'Priests of the tribe of Levi' certainly *may* have ministered at Shiloh and other places. I see no reason to believe that they actually *did* so minister, as a tribe specially set apart for such services, till the time of David. See *P*.V.Chap.xv.

[83] This is said with reference particularly to Prof. Dozy's view as to the ceremonies at Shiloh, and at the Gilgal, which he compares with those of the Meccan festival, *p*.125.

Human sacrifices were offered on special occasions in order to pacify the angry JHVH : on the gibbet, [N.xxv.4, 2S.xxi.9,] or on the altar, [*P*.V.Chap.xx,] the victims were put to death. Prostitution in honour of the Deity was no uncommon thing [*P*.V.371]. At the Gilgal, as appears by the excellent discovery of Prof. Dozy, were celebrated rude military reminiscences of the Conquest of the Land.[84] In short, we find everywhere the traces of very arbitrary JHVH-worship.

91. Nothing was more natural than this. We know not what was the religion of the Israelites before they received JHVH-ism from the hand of Moses,[85]—to what extent the worship of sacred trees and stones, the adoration of the Baalim or different kinds of Gods, sacrifices and solemnities, were practised among them. But we can scarcely suppose their religious

---

[84] This view as to the meaning of the Feast at the Gilgal appears to me very doubtful. The Israelites, no doubt, had some conflicts with the Canaanites before they made good their footing in the land; and the Feast in question *may* have been instituted to commemorate the termination of these struggles. But there is no substantial proof that there was really any great 'Conquest' of the land under Joshua, about half the account of whose doings is written by the Deuteronomist (*P*.V.5) in the reign of Josiah, eight centuries after the Exodus; and the very name of Joshua is never once mentioned by any one of the Psalmists or Prophets. When, again, we remember that the Israelites did *not* complete at all in that age the conquest of the land, as we learn from the Book of Joshua itself, xv.63,xvi.10,xvii.12,16, and especially xviii.2,3, see also Ju.i.19,21,27-36,—that the more truly historical Book of Judges exhibits them frequently in a state of servitude and distress—that 'the five lords of the Philistines, and all the Canaanites, and the Sidonians, and the Hivites, that dwell in Mount Lebanon' were left to 'prove Israel,' Ju.iii.4,—that 'the children of Israel dwelt among the Canaanites, Hittites, and Amorites, and Perizzites, and Hivites, and Jebusites, and they took their daughters to be their wives, and gave their daughters to their sons, and served their gods,' *v*.5,6,—it seems unlikely that the 'Feast at the Gilgal' should have commemorated yearly their '*Conquest* of the Land,' though it may have celebrated their *Settlement* in it, and may have been reproduced in the Meccan Festival.

[85] Here, again, is the great assumption. What proof is there that the Israelites received JHVH-ism 'from the hand of Moses'? Everything seems rather, in our view, to show that they received it, or, rather, that they received the first principles of a more pure and spiritual religion,—the worship of JEHOVAH,—'from the hand of' *Samuel*, who is coupled so suggestively with Moses in Jer.xv.1.

ideas and forms of worship to have been very much developed. Further, we can scarcely suppose that they had *unity* of worship: although, naturally, there would exist considerable *uniformity* among tribes connected with one another by ties of blood and unity of interest.

92. In the wilderness, however, they recognise the God of their deliverer (Moses), and his tribe or family as their God, the God of Gods. But, for all this, the religious and moral principles of JHVH-ism, or, if it is preferred, of the religion of Moses, did not penetrate into them. The rude warriors had probably something else to do than to get themselves instructed in matters of religion. And so each maintained the superstitions, the religious usages, which he previously had, while together *with* these or *in* these all he worshipped JHVH, sware by JHVH, and went to war in the name of JHVH.[86]

93. When, however, Israel conquered Canaan, they found there various tribes, whose worship undoubtedly had much agreement with their own in some points,[87] while in other

[86] It seems to me that EWALD's idea, that JHVH was the Deity worshipped in the family or tribe of Moses *before* the Exodus, is highly improbable, (see this point discussed fully in *P.V.*Chap.xix,) and that there is no real proof whatever that they 'worshipped JHVH' in the wilderness, or 'sware by Him,' or 'went to fight in His Name,'—still less that under the eye of Moses himself, (for forty years long, says the traditionary view, though critics would greatly diminish this time,) they practised this supposed mixture of JHVH-worship and idolatry. This assumption rests upon a belief in the historical value of some of the details in the Pentateuch—(as, for instance, the name, 'Jochebed,' of the mother of Moses, which is compounded with 'Jehovah,' and, if genuine, would show that the name was known and commonly used *before* its revelation to Moses,)—while others, and these some of the main portions of the narrative, as E.vi.2–7, are altogether rejected.

[87] That the Israelites in Egypt may have retained something of the old Sun-worship, which their fathers probably practised 'beyond the (flood) Euphrates,' Jo.xxiv.14, and may have found the same again in full development, when they entered the land of Canaan, is certainly possible. But the Hebrew tradition appears distinctly to fix the time of their first making acquaintance with the name JHVH, as contemporaneous with that of the Exodus, E.vi.2–7 (*P.V.* 318); and the absence of any names compounded with JHVH (except Joshua and Jochebed) in the Pentateuch itself seems to confirm this. The residual historical fact, as we have

respects it varied greatly from it. In many districts Israel was closely mixed with the Canaanites, and naturally these latter received in consequence JHVH-ism,[88]—as, for instance, the Nethinim of later centuries, the Gibeonites, 'Solomon's servants.' But they imported also their own religious forms and ideas into the Israelitish worship, which happened the more easily, inasmuch as these were little defined and very arbitrary.

94. The JHVH-ism of Joshua's troopers was a name, and nothing more.[89] And what strange abortions may be generated, when a people that conquers a land brings thither a religion which it understands but little itself, the history of Christendom and Islam shows in numerous instances. Thus there arose in Canaan the most singular medley, which, however opposed,

---

said (note [22.1]), which lies at the basis of this tradition, (if we reject the notion of the supernatural revelation to Moses), would appear to be no other than this, that they learned it first from their contact with the tribes of Canaan; unless any will adopt the idea of EWALD, which seems to us very unnatural, that JHVH was worshipped by name before the Exodus, but privately in the family or tribe of Moses, and by him was first imparted to Israel at the time of their wanderings.

[88] On our view, of course, the Israelites received JHVH-ism from the Canaanites. Where is there any indication that the 'Nethinim,' 'Gibeonites,' and 'Solomon's servants,' received it from the Israelites?

[89] It would seem to be incredible that the worship of JHVH in Israel,—after the schooling of Moses and Joshua, and the ministrations of Aaron and Eleazar,—nay, under the actual superintendence of Phinehas,—should have been so 'little defined' and so 'very arbitrary,' as Dr. OORT supposes, or that 'the JHVH-ism of Joshua's troopers should have been a name, and nothing more,' if there is any substantial truth in the story of the Book of Joshua. How, if JHVH-ism was only a name among Joshua's troopers, did they come to influence so powerfully the neighbouring tribes, as Dr. OORT supposes them to have done? But, surely, Joshua, Eleazar, Phinehas, and 'the elders who outlived Joshua,' must have understood fully the religion of the wilderness; and their influence must have lasted—according to the Bible for nearly a century, but, at all events,—for a considerable time after the Exodus.

In short, it seems to us, that the acquisition by the Hebrews of the worship of JHVH from the tribes of Canaan is very intelligible and natural, if there is any truth in the facts set forth by MOVERS as to the Phœnician worship of the Sun under the name IAO; and so also is the fact, which the history discloses, that, as time advanced, their Great Prophets, divinely taught and enlightened, sought to purify their worship, while still they retained the Name. But it is far more difficult to conceive the course of development, which Dr. OORT's theory supposes.

lasted till the Captivity: while a Jeremiah could exclaim, ii.28, xi.13,—

'As many as thy towns, O Judah! so are thy gods!'

Nevertheless, it remained always the people of JHVH.[90]

95. Yet in the midst of this mixture of religions there was working a little seed, spiritual children of Moses. In the spirit of the Law of the Ten Commandments [91] they sought to reform the worship of Israel. JHVH was for them the *only* Deity: it was unlawful to make an image of Him: the oath taken in His Name was sacred: the observance of the Sabbath was pleasing to Him,—respect for elders, and moral virtue, His Will.

96. Their activity remained long unnoticed. But this spiritual seed acquired influence by degrees, and opposed more openly, as time advanced, all which conflicted with their higher conceptions of JHVH-worship. With that view, they tried to get into their hands the priestly offices, and to prevent all private worship.[92] Gradually, all feasts, usages, and solemnities,

[90] Yes—from the time that it became 'a people' at all, and became also 'the people of JHVH,' in Samuel's days.

[91] The 'Ten Commandments' date, as we have said (note [20]), from the age of Josiah. Jehovah was 'the Elohim,' the Great God, the God of Israel, to the earlier writers of the Pentateuch,—but not the *only* God (note [71]). It was not forbidden to make an *image* for purposes of worship in *their* days; for we see that 'teraphim' are mentioned without any mark of censure in G.xxxi.19, xxxv.2,4, Ju.xvii.5, xviii.20, 1S.xix.13, as is a graven or molten image in Ju.xvii.3,4, xviii.31. On these points the Pentateuch, as we now have it, betrays the developments of a later age.

According to our view, the 'spiritual seed' in question, which worked continually in the endeavour to elevate and spiritualise the worship of JHVH in Israel, was the series of Prophets who followed in the footsteps of Samuel. The *modesty* of the latter referred his own work, in the Elohistic document, to the activity of Moses. But Samuel was himself the Prophet—not Moses—who received the Divine illumination, and laid the first principles of a spiritual religion, the worship of JEHOVAH, in Israel.

[92] This may have been the case in Solomon's time, when Zadok,—probably one of the School of Samuel,—by taking part with the young king against his elder brother Adonijah, 1K.i.8, &c., secured the expulsion of his older fellow-priest, Abiathar, 1K.ii.35, and the appointment of himself in charge of the Sanctuary at Jerusalem

which the people kept in honour of JHVH, but which in their view were unlawful,[93] were declared to be idolatrous. It is obvious that the worship of the Baalim was an offence to them. Yet is there no indication that before Ahab's time Baal was an idolatrous name.[94]

97. Idolatrous, or anti-JHVH-istic, the Baal-worship could not have been, until the worshipping of Baal appeared as something anti-national : and that did not happen till after Solomon's days.[95] But the grounds for it were already laid in his time. In Tyre, as we know, Hiram reigned simultaneously with David and Solomon, under whom that state attained an unprecedented glory. Hiram employed for the maintenance of his authority the same means as his friend Solomon, *viz.* the erection of a splendid Temple for the national Deity, the Baal

---

—that is, first of the Tabernacle, and then of the Temple. But it does not seem that the Priests in later days—except, perhaps, Hilkiah in Josiah's time—were Reformers of the worship of JHVH. There were some spiritually-minded *Prophets* all along, who laboured for this, and Jeremiah was of a priestly family: but these were very commonly opposed to the *Priests*, as well as to other, non-reforming, *Prophets*: see Jer.i.18, ii.8,26, v.31, especially xx.1,2, xxvi.7,8,11, xxix.26,27.

[93] That is, as we may suppose, all worship of JHVH, which was conducted after the idolatrous fashions of the tribes around them.

[94] But see note [62], where some indications are given of the existence of a *dislike* for the use of the name 'Baal' in connection with JHVH, even as early as the time of David.

[95] The worshipping of the Baal was never anti-JHVH-istic, but it was anti-Jehov-istic,—that is, it was opposed to the spirit of the Reformers, Samuel and his followers. The attempt to centralise the worship of Jehovah at Jerusalem, in David's time and Solomon's, was made with a view to the suppression of the irregular JHVH-worship, in different parts of the land, gradually and without violence; but it utterly failed, and, before long, the worship in the Temple itself degenerated into Baal-worship. Even before 'Solomon's days,' however, as we have seen (note [62]), there are signs that the use of the name 'Baal' in connection with Jehovah-worship was objected to,—not by the people generally, but by the Psalmists and pious Prophets—as injurious to the progress of true religion in the land, dishonouring to the true Lord, the 'Husband,' of Israel, and, therefore, in the highest sense of the word, 'anti-national.' With the people at large, however, no doubt, as Dr. Oort says, the worship of the Baal, that is, of JHVH, was not 'anti-national,' until the time of Ahab, when a new form of idolatry was sought to be introduced—the worship of the 'Tyrian Baal.'

of Tyre, Melkarth [מֶלֶךְ קֶרֶת, *melech kereth*, 'king of the city'],
the worship of which deity seems to have been greatly extended
and developed at that period.

98. We are told, for instance, of Hiram, (MENANDER in
JOSEPH., *Ant.*VIII.v.3, and *contr.Ap.*I.18,*) first, that he
placed a golden pillar [? Ashera or Phallus] before the Temple
of Jupiter Olympius—then, that he overthrew the old sanctuaries and consecrated enclosures (τέμενος) for Herakles and
Astarte, and built new temples upon them, of which the roofs
were made of cedar,—lastly, that he was the first to celebrate
the Feast of the Resurrection of Herakles (πρῶτός τε τοῦ
Ἡρακλέους ἔγερσιν ἐποιήσατο). The worship of Herakles or
Melkarth had much in common with Sun-worship[96] (*comp.*
J. O. MÜLLER in HERZ. *Real-Enc.* I.p.639-641): and to this
belonged among other things the Festival in Spring when he
awaked again, to which, perhaps, Elijah alluded in his mocking
words on Carmel, 1K.xviii.27 —

'Cry aloud, for he is God: either he is talking, or he is pursuing, or he is in
a journey, or peradventure he sleepeth, and must be awaked.'

99. This worship was introduced into Israel under Ahab.
This king married Jezebel, daughter of the Sidonian, or rather
Tyrian,† king Eth-Baal, and built in Samaria a splendid temple
for 'the Baal,' that is, for 'the Tyrian Baal,' Melkarth, erected

[96] The worship of the 'Tyrian Baal' had, of course, a close connection with
Sun-worship, for Herakles *was* the Sun: see note [16]. The 'Feast of the Resur-
rection' of Herakles was the celebration of the birth of the new year after the
death of the old: and this festival, too, existed in the worship of the *Syrian* Baal,
'Adonis,' who was said to have 'risen again from the dead on the third day': see
P.V.*App.*III.27.

* These quotations do not agree strictly in their statements: that in the Antiquities is the most accurate.—OORT.

† In this way is usually corrected the notice in 1K.xvi.31, in which Jezebel is
called a *Sidonian*. The reason for this is that in Ahab's time (according to
JOSEPHUS, as above) Ethbaal reigned in *Tyre*. To this it may be added, that the
Baal-worship was evidently paramount, even if coupled with an *Astarte*-worship:
whereas Astarte would certainly have been the chief deity, if Jezebel had come
from Sidon, 1K.xi.5, 2K.xxiii.13.—OORT.

near it a memorial-stone (מַצֵּבָה), which his son put-away, 2K.iii.2, and a pillar (ashera), 1K.xvi.31,32, which was left standing when Jehu destroyed the Temple, 2K.x.18-27.

100. And now began a violent opposition to the Baal. The zealous servants of JHVH, headed by Elijah or Elisha, did their best, and JHVH triumphed when Jehu appeared on the stage: though it would seem that in this struggle Prophetism also had exhausted its strength. The contest between the Baal and the Prophets is graphically described in 1K.xviii,xix, which is not an historical record in the strict sense of the word, but gives us in the person of Elijah a picture of Prophetdom, exactly as, amidst the persecutions of the Court-Party, it maintained the honour of JHVH. *See* Prof. KUENEN's Art. on 'The Prophet Elijah,' in *Niew en Oud*, 1864, V.*p*.107-144.

101. Thus the name 'Baal'—or rather 'the Baal'—became an idolatrous name. Henceforward, the word might be used in two senses, *with the article* as a designation of Melkarth,[97] and *in the plural* (Baalim), as denoting gods honoured together with JHVH.[98] This double use of the word we find also in Hosea. In ii.1-13 he mentions with abhorrence the idolatry of Israel, as practised under Ahab and his successors, the remains of which probably still existed here and there: [99]—

[97] But what then is the meaning of ἡ Βάαλ, used invariably in the LXX translation of Jeremiah and Zephaniah (note [17])? Is it not probable that the LXX, at all events, understood 'the Baal' to be used also, both before and after Ahab's days, of 'the heifer,' ἡ δάμαλις, Tob.i.5, 2K.x.29, which was the symbol of the old Phœnician Baal?

[98] In our view, of course, the 'Baalim' did not 'denote gods honoured *together with* JHVH'—but represented JHVH, 'the Baal,' himself.

[99] But Hosea wrote about a *century* after Jehu had *rooted out utterly*, it would seem, the worship of the *Tyrian* Baal. Surely the words in 2K.x.18-28 imply this. We read here that Jehu summoned '*all the prophets* of the Baal, *all his servants*, and *all his priests*,—let none be wanting—whosoever shall be wanting he shall not live,' *v.*19. 'And Jehu sent throughout all Israel; and *all the worshippers* of the Baal came, so that there was not a man left that came not,' *v.*21. And then after the massacre of all these, it is added, *v.*26-28:—

'And they brought forth the image out of the house of the Baal, and brake down the house of the Baal, and made it a draught-house unto this day. *Thus*

'They have used the corn, must, and oil, which JHVH gave them, for the Baal.' *v.*8.

'And I will visit upon them the days of the Baalim, wherein she burnt incense to them . . . and forgat me, saith JHVH.' *v.*13.

'After that JHVH will again be gracious to them, and they shall no more call him ' my (Baal) Lord,' but ' my (Ish) Husband ' ; and JHVH will take-away the names of the Baalim out of their mouths, and they shall no more be remembered by their name.' *v.*16,17.

It is plain that mention is here made of a kind of JHVH-worship, to which the Prophet objects.

102. So, again, Melkárth ('the Baal') is indicated in Ho.xiii.1 : [100] and in xi.2 'the Baalim' are mentioned. Nothing is more natural than that the Tyrian Baal should have brought his more innocent brothers in Israel into still greater discredit than as yet had attached to them, even in the view of the most highly advanced Israelites.[101]

103. In Judah the worship of the Tyrian Baal was introduced when Athaliah was queen, 2K.xi.18. But, when Joash ascended the throne, it was again abolished. The expression 'the Baal' was, however, in Judah synonymous, not only with every kind of idolatry, but also with *every kind of unlawful JHVH-worship*,[102] to which the Prophets quite as strongly objected.

Jehu destroyed the Baal out of Israel. Howbeit, as to the sins of Jeroboam, the son of Nebat, who made Israel to sin, Jehu departed not from after them, the golden heifers (αἱ δαμάλεις αἱ χρυσαῖ) in Bethel and in Dan.'

It seems plain that no 'remains' of the worship of the *Tyrian* Baal were left in Israel: while yet Jehu clave to the worship of the *Syrian* Baal, JHVH, to which his people were of old attached, and whose symbol was the heifer (ἡ Βάαλ ἡ δάμαλις, Tob.i.5). It is *this* Baal, as we suppose, to whom Hosea refers in ii.8 ; and accordingly the LXX uses here ἡ Βάαλ, while throughout the story of Jehu and the Tyrian Baal, in 2K.x.18-28, only ὁ Βάαλ is used. And so we understand 'the Baalim' in Hos.ii.13,17, as referring also to the representatives of JHVH throughout the land—'a kind of JHVH-worship' to which, no doubt, 'the Prophet objected.'

[100] No! here also the reference is to 'the heifer,' and the LXX has ἡ Βάαλ.

[101] This is probably true. But from the times of Samuel downwards those 'brethren' had been regarded with suspicion by the more enlightened men in Israel, and had probably long ceased to be considered by them as 'innocent': see note [62].

[102] Exactly so : this entirely accords with our view that the idolatries in Judah

104. Thus Jeremiah says that the Israelites worshipped the Baalim 'whom their fathers taught them,' ix.14,[103] and thus he plainly recognises that this worship was a part of the old religion.[104] But 'burning incense to the Baal' stands with him in the same category with 'following after other gods,' vii.9, of which gods, according to *v*.18, and xliv.17–19, the 'Queen of Heaven' seems to have had the foremost place.[105] If

were almost all of this kind, *viz.* idolatrous JHVH-worship. Accordingly, as we have seen (note [97]), the LXX invariably use ἡ Βάαλ in their translation of Jeremiah and Zephaniah, though they use always ὁ βάαλ of the Tyrian Baal, 1K. xvi.31,32, xviii.22,26,40, xix.18, 2K.iii.2, x.18–28, xi.18. But ὁ βάαλ might also be used for the *Phœnician* Baal with reference to the *Deity*, and not to the form of his *idol*, the heifer: and so we find it used both *before* the introduction of the worship of the Tyrian Baal, Ju.ii.13, vi.25,28,30,31,32, viii.33, x.10, and *after* its abolition, 2K.xvii.16, xxiii.4,5.

[103] True: but he also says, xxiii.27, 'their fathers have forgotten my Name through the Baal,' that is, as we understand it, had forgotten the true meaning of the Name, had used it as JHVH, the name of the Baal, not as JEHOVAH, the Name of the Living God; and from this text it might be argued that they knew *first* the spiritual meaning of the Name, and abandoned it for the carnal. And, no doubt, the Prophet means to charge them with this, assuming, of course, as he might, the general truth of the story of the Exodus. But the statement would also be substantially true, if he referred to the time of Samuel, when the people 'put away the Baalim and the Astartes,' at the Prophet's exhortation, 'and served Jehovah only,' 1S.vii.4. This was the starting-point, as we suppose, of the worship of JEHOVAH, whose Name, in its higher spiritual meaning, was in that age, as we suppose, *first* declared to them, by the *oral* teaching of the Prophet and his disciples, supported by the *written* documents which they composed for them, *e.g.* the narrative of the Exodus; *comp.* E.iii.13–15, vi.2–7, &c. From this knowledge of the Name they fell away, seduced, as Jeremiah says, xii.14, by 'the evil neighbours that touched their inheritance,' and taught by them to 'swear by the Baal,' *v*.16.

[104] Certainly: the worship of the Baalim was part of the old worship of JHVH, which had prevailed in Israel, more or less, ever since the time of their entrance into Canaan, that is, in fact, ever since the Exodus. But this worship was all along, as we believe, regarded by devout persons as 'idolatrous,' though at first, as late as the time of David, JEHOVAH was regarded by good men as 'the Baal' of Israel (note [62]). But very soon this use of the name 'Baal' was laid aside, and confined to the idolatrous worship of JHVH.

[105] The worship of the 'Queen of Heaven' was a *new* worship, part of the *astrological* worship of the Sun, Moon, and Planets, recently introduced from Chaldæa, and the adoption of which, therefore, was rightly spoken of as a 'following after other gods.' But, that Jeremiah does not, as Dr. OORT supposes, use the phrase 'burn incense to the Baal,' as a synonym for *any* species of idolatry, or for 'lying

he declares of the Prophets of Samaria, xxiii.13, and of those of Jerusalem, ii.8, that they prophesied by 'the Baal,' he indicates by this—not idolatry, strictly speaking, but—'lying prophecy' of all kinds.[106] We have seen above (17–29) how deeply JHVH-ism had sunk into the heart of the people of the northern kingdom.[107] And this was not less the case in Judah, as the well-known narrative in Jer.xxvi teaches us. 'The Baal' is, consequently, a synonym with him for 'the spirit of of lying.'[108]

105. I hope that I have here indicated sufficiently the connection between the worship of the Baalim and that of JHVH. We must now pay a visit to the Temple of Mecca, in order to see if the discovery there made overthrows our conclusion as to the history of Baal-worship, as gathered from the O.T.

---

prophecy of all kinds'—that he refers here, as elsewhere, to the heifer-worship, the idolatrous worship of JHVH,—seems to be shown by the LXX using here ἡ βάαλ.

[106] I cannot agree with this view, but believe that Jeremiah refers always literally, in the expression 'the Baal (ἡ βάαλ),' to the idolatrous worship of JHVH under the form of a heifer.

[107] That is, of course, not JEHOV-ism, but idolatrous JHVH-ism, the worship of the Syrian Baal.

[108] For the reasons above given (note [106]), I cannot assent to this statement.

N.B. In *het Menschenoffer in Israel*, p.134, Dr. OORT explains Jer.ii.23 by supposing that in Jeremiah's days the *name* 'Baal' was in discredit even with the multitude,—which appears also from the fact that in that age *Beth*-Meon was used, Jer.xliii.24, for *Baal*-Meon, (though Ezekiel has the old form, xxv.9,) and Kirjath-Jearim, Jer.xxvi.20, for Baal of Judah. 'Hence the people said truly that they were not defiled through the Baal. But there was no reason to boast of this: what they did was no better than the old Baal-worship.'

This agrees completely with our own view. The great body of the people objected to the worship of 'the Baal,' *i.e.* of the *Tyrian* Baal, which Athaliah, Jezebel's daughter, introduced into Jerusalem; and 'all the people of the land went into the house of the Baal, and brake it down; his altars and his images brake they in pieces thoroughly, and slew Matthan, the priest of the Baal, before his altars.' 2K.xi.18. But still 'the high-places were not taken away; the people still sacrificed and burnt incense in the high-places,' 2K.xii.3: that is, the people still worshipped JHVH, the *Syrian* Baal, as of old. From this time, however, they may have ceased to call JHVH 'the Baal,' whence their plea, that in Jeremiah's days they were not defiled with 'Baalim.'

SECTION III.

THE RELIGION OF THE EXPATRIATED SIMEONITES.

106. PROF. DOZY thinks that *the chief Deity worshipped at Mecca was 'the Baal,' and that, next to him, JHVH was worshipped in the form of a he-goat.*

With reference to this I wish to show that, if the supposed he-goats are the only proof of the existence of JHVH-ism[109] in Arabia, we may say that this religion has quietly disappeared without leaving a trace behind it; since these can scarcely be called images of JHVH.

107. In the Temple at Mecca were two gold gazelles, which the Jews, when expelled by the Chozaha, two centuries after Christ, buried with some breast-plates and swords in a dried-up well. These, however, were dug up a few generations before the time of Mohammed; and one of them was placed in the treasury of Hobal, [the idol worshipped at Mecca before Ma-

---

[109] The Simeonites, as we suppose, in common with Prof. Dozy and Dr. OORT, emigrated to Arabia *about the beginning of David's reign*, and carried to Mecca the worship of 'the Baal' of Syria. But the mysterious name of this Deity, from which, as we suppose, the name 'JHVH' originated, appears to have been chiefly in use at Byblus, &c., among the tribes of the *north* of Canaan (see *P.V.App.*III.10,11,&c.); and the name 'Jehovah' had only been recently introduced into the religious history of Israel, when the Simeonites left their abodes in the extreme *south* of the land, and certainly, to judge from the Psalms, had not yet become familiar. In fact, in that age, David could still call his son Baalyadah. It is possible, therefore, that the Simeonites may *not* have carried with them the name JHVH at all. At any rate, no trace of the name is found at Mecca: which fact (so far as it goes) is an additional argument against the *Divine* origin of the name as described in the Pentateuch, and against EWALD's view of its having been introduced in the *Mosaic age*; since in either case the Simeonites must have known and used it: see note[129].

hommed's time, of which more presently,] the other used to adorn the door of the Temple. Prof. Dozy, p.41,43,101,102, thinks that these were not gazelles, but he-goats, and finds in them images of JHVH, because it is said of Jeroboam, 2Ch.xi.15, that he 'appointed priests of the high-places and of the *he-goats* (שְׂעִירִים), and of the steers * [110] which he had made,'—

and because also in L.xvii.7 it is forbidden to sacrifice to the 'he-goats.' From these passages it is inferred that JHVH was worshipped under the form of a he-goat, as well as under that of a steer. Both images are of Egyptian origin: in fact, the formula used of the steer, 1K.xii.28,*comp*.E.xxxii.4,Neh.ix.18,†—

'This is thy God, O'Israel, who brought thee out of the land of Egypt'—

shows that this worship already existed in the wilderness.[111] The steer is the Egyptian Apis.

[110] It would rather seem that Jeroboam's calves were not *steers*, but *heifers*. The LXX distinctly implies this in 1K.xii.28,29,32, as also in 2K.x.29, xvii.16, Hos.x.5, (where reference is made to them,) since it speaks of ἡ δάμαλις, αἱ δαμάλεις; and so too in Tob.i.5 we have Jeroboam's calf referred to as ἡ Βάαλ ἡ δάμαλις. In 2Ch.xi.15, xiii.8, it is true, the LXX speaks of them as οἱ μόσχοι, and so it refers to one of them as ὁ μόσχος in Hos.viii.5,6, xiii.2, as well as in the story of Aaron's calf, E.xxxii.4,8,19,20,24,35, and in D.ix.16,21,Neh.ix.18,Ps.cvi(cv).19, where Aaron's calf is also spoken of. In all cases the Hebrew text has עֵגֶל, עֲגָלִים, not עֶגְלָה.—except in Hos.x.5, where we have עֶגְלוֹת, 'heifers': but this last seems to be decisive; since עֵגֶל and μόσχος, 'calf,' might be used to include 'heifer,' but עֶגְלוֹת, δαμάλεις, 'heifers,' could not be employed for 'steers.'

I conclude, therefore, that Jeroboam's calf—and probably Aaron's also—was a 'heifer,' not a 'steer'; but I retain, of course, Dr. OORT's word in the Text.

[111] According to our view, the use of these words certainly does not show that

---

* This is usually translated 'calves,' and Prof. Dozy adopts this, p.41, especially because the Egyptian Apis is called a calf (μόσχος). This seems to me to be nothing to the purpose. However, the Hebrew עֵגֶל denotes, not a *calf*, but a *young bullock*. In all cases an עֶגְלָה [or עֵגֶל, Jer.xxxi.18,] is used for ploughing and threshing, Ju.xiv.18, Hos.x.11; [D.xxi.3,] which work is not done with calves. See J. G. MÜLLER in *Herz. Real Enc.*vii.214,215.—OORT. [See also note [110].]

† In the first two of these passages the verb is used in the *plural*, so that it seems to be used of 'Gods,' as if to avoid giving offence.—OORT. [But see G.xx.13, xxxi.53, D.iv.7, 28.vii.23, 1K.xix.2,xx.10, where a plural verb or adjective is used with Elohim. GEIGER, *Urschrift*, p.283–288, regards all these plurals as corrections by later Scribes, made for religious reasons.—*Ed.*]

108. Let us see what this amounts to. No appeal can be made in proof of this to 2Ch.xi.15. In the first place, the writer here does not at all explain what he understands by שְׂעִירִים, 'he-goats' [E.V. 'devils.'] The connection of them with high-places and images of steers does not throw much light upon the matter. That he intends by them something *made*, does not follow from his words; since the addition, 'which he had made,' refers, perhaps, only to the steers. But in any case he understands by them a worship to which priests belonged.

109. What he thought of it, however, is not of much consequence for us, since in his time (77) very little indeed was understood of the old state of things. His account also is very far from being accurate; for he represents the matter as if in *the northern kingdom* 'high-places and שְׂעִי and steers' were honoured, while in *Judah* no such abominations were to be found; and in so doing he very much forgets himself. Further, he opposes to these 'high-places, שְׂעִירִים, and steers,' the worship of JHVH, as if everything besides this last was idolatry.[112]

110. Thus the only passage, which can give us any informa-

---

the heifer-worship existed already in the wilderness. But it does seem to show distinctly that the 'heifer'—the symbol of 'the Baal,' ἡ Βάαλ ἡ δάμαλις, Tob.i.5—was intended to represent JHVH, who for, at least, a century and a half—from Samuel's days to those of Jeroboam—was popularly said to have 'brought them forth out of the land of Egypt.' And so observes KEIL on 1K.xii.26-29, (KEIL and BERTHEAU, *Eng. Ed.* i.p.219)—'From this verbal reference to that fact [Aaron's calf in the wilderness] it appears that the worship of the calves was no proper idolatry, from which also it is always distinguished in these Books, as in the Prophets Hosea and Amos; but it would seem that under the symbol of the calves Jehovah [? JHVH] was worshipped.'

[112] Rather, he opposes to them the worship of JEHOVAH, which was existing fully developed in the Chronicler's day. Dr. OORT means to say, of course, that the heifer-worship and the worship on high-places was not opposed to the worship of JHVH in Jeroboam's days,—was, in fact, identical with it. And this is true. But even a Prophet of that time would have regarded such worship as opposed to JEHOVAH-worship, and therefore idolatrous: and the Chronicler, who had only JEHOVAH-worship before his eyes, (JHVH-worship having long ago disappeared,) would, of course, speak of it as rank idolatry.

tion as to the existence of images of JHVH in the form of a he-goat, is L.xvii.7. But, whoever reads this passage in connection with the context before and after, will see that it will be very difficult indeed to discover this here. In this passage, indeed, it is prescribed that, whoever would slay an animal, must do it before the Sanctuary,—

to the end that they may bring their sacrifices, which they bring upon the face of the field, to JHVH, and no more to the שְׂעִירִים, after which they have gone a whoring.'

But it is plain that here nothing is said about images of JHVH: for the worship, to which the legislator objects, is emphatically distinguished from the worship of JHVH.*

111. Besides, supposing even that Prof. Dozy's explanation were true, what would the expression 'upon the face of the field' denote? We do not know what was the practice of the Israelites in slaughtering an animal. But the language makes it probable that mention is here made of a worshipping of field-spirits or wood-spirits, Satyrs, to whom a libation of blood or something of that kind was brought.

112. The same word, שָׂעִיר, may also have this meaning of 'field-spirit, Satyr,' in Is.xiii.21,xxxiv.14, where it is said of creatures thus designated, that they hop round in old ruins, in company with ostriches and other animals, and cry one to another.† Whenever שָׂעִיר is used for a 'he-goat,' it is always coupled with עִזִּים, G.xxxvii.31, L.iv.23,xvi.8, N.vii.87; and so, too, a she-goat is called שְׂעִירַת עִזִּים, L.iv.28,v.6. This addition is only wanting in cases where the full expression precedes, and where misunderstanding is impossible, as in L.iv.24,xvi

---

* In later times an unlawful JHVH-worship was called idolatry: but L.xvii is an old pre-Deuteronomistic Law, referred to in D.xii.15,21.—OORT. [I do not believe that L.xvii is *much* older than Deuteronomy. But I hold that in all ages, from the time of Samuel downwards, the more enlightened Prophets regarded as idolatrous all that was not agreeable (in their view) with the worship of JEHOVAH.—*Ed.*]

† See with regard to such kinds of superstition among the later Jews GES. *in Is.* p.464.465,915–919.—OORT.

(*passim*). The formula cannot be translated into our tongue: the word (*geiten-bok*) 'he-goat of the goats,' contains, of course, a strange pleonasm. But the Israelites evidently knew of *other* שְׂעִירִים, besides those belonging to flocks. In the above-quoted passages of Isaiah the Greek translators found already *demons* (δαιμόνια), and in L.xvii they write μάταια ['absurdities']. The usual Hebrew word for he-goat is שָׂעִיר.

113. There is, consequently, not a single evidence to be produced for the view that JHVH was worshipped in Israel under the form of a he-goat. And thus there is also no reason for seeing 'images of JHVH' in the two animals of the Meccan Temple,—which, moreover, the Arabians regard, not as he-goats, but as *gazelles*. There is, again, something very strange in the circumstance that there should have been *two* copies of the animal. Lastly, since tradition does not speak of them as images of deities, but places them in the same category with breast-plates and swords, we may quietly consider them as set aside.

114. Here we might rest satisfied, and, leaving the gold gazelles to their fate, might go on at once to speak about Hobal. But Prof. Dozy, on the occasion of discussing the he-goats, has treated also the question of the steer-worship, and declared it to be of *Egyptian* origin. I may be allowed to bring forward one or two considerations bearing on this point.

115. What real ground is there for the constantly repeated asseveration, that the worship of JHVH, under the form of a steer, was of Egyptian origin? We do not know whether in very ancient times such a relationship existed between the Israelites and Egyptians, that they formed one people, and thus worshipped the same Deities. But the only reminiscence of Israel, which we can call historical, is this, that the people was *enslaved* in Egypt and *miserable*. See this described in vivid colours by Ezekiel, xvi.4-6. The Egyptian tradition,

which connects Israel with *leprosy*, agrees with this. Israel is never spoken of as an *Egyptian* tribe.

116. Now, I conceive that an oppressed people will never adopt the religion of its oppressors, unless it becomes absorbed in them and loses its nationality, as was the case with the Nethinim in Israel. Israel did not become Egyptian: instead of this, it cut itself loose from Egypt: whatever was indigenous there, must in consequence have been hateful in Israel. At the same time, we do not wish to deny that some religious usages of Egypt might—by means either of Egyptians who became proselytes, and so became Israelites, or of Hebrews, who stood on a friendly footing with Egyptians,—have slipped into the worship of Israel. But this can only have happened with petty details, confined within narrow limits. A religion, which the Israelites knew to be Egyptian, could hardly have become national in Israel.*

117. If for a moment we assume that the account in E.xxxii, according to which JHVH was worshipped even in the wilderness under the form of a steer, is historical—(a point which is exceedingly doubtful)—still it is not allowable to see in this an Apis-worship or an imitation of it. What, truly, would have been the meaning of that exclamation,—

'Behold thy God, O Israel, who brought thee out of Egypt!'

if that God had been Apis? Had, then, the God of the Egyptians rescued them out of the hand of *his own worshippers?* To this it may be added that Apis was a *living* steer.[113]

118. It is difficult to prove that the word *Abbir* (אַבִּיר) 'the

---

[113] Dr. OORT's argument here seems decisive. Clearly, this account of Aaron's calf—or heifer—was written (of course, long after the Mosaic time) with reference to the heifer-worship in Israel, which they had learned from the tribes of Canaan.

---

* When Ezekiel declares, xx.7,8, that Israel was polluted with the Egyptian (גִּלּוּלִים) idols, he probably did not follow in this an historical tradition, but merely assumed this, according to the principle *cujus regio ejus religio*. See 1S.xxvi.19, R.i.15, ii.12, D.iv.28.—OORT.

strong one,' is no other than the Egyptian *Api* (=Apis), [as Prof. Dozy supposes.] Israel could not have adopted this word *directly and consciously*, without recognising itself as an Egyptian tribe and worshipping the Egyptian Deity: but in that case it would have worshipped the *living* steer. Did it slip into the Hebrew tongue *unconsciously*?* That is not at all probable: for first the final *r* is wanting in the Egyptian, and then the vowels correspond exactly, whereas in other cases these are generally modified, when a word passes from one language to another.

119. The root of the word אָבִיר seems to have been lost. But in one of the oldest records[114] in the Hebrew tongue which we possess, the Song of Deborah, אַבִּיר is used already in the sense of 'hero,' Ju.v.22. When, therefore, Jeremiah some centuries afterwards, says to the Egyptians, 'Thy אַבִּיר,' [E.V. 'thy mighty-ones,' but note the *keri*, and the singular verbs,] this signifies merely 'Thy Mighty-one,'—probably, with an allusion to Apis, which indeed the LXX finds in it, xlvi(xxvi).15, [Διατί ἔφυγεν ἀπὸ σοῦ ὁ Ἆπις.]

120. The steer-worship in Israel can hardly have been of Egyptian origin; and it makes nothing to the purpose whether Jeroboam came out of Egypt at the time when he introduced it, or not (THENIUS, *Buch der Kon. p.*183). No prince could introduce a religion among his people with good effect, unless there existed previously among the people an inclination for it: such a novelty could not be forced upon them, says Prof. Dozy, *p.*83, very justly.

121. The representation of JHVH in the form of a steer may very well have been a purely Israelitish symbol.[115] The steer is among a bucolic people a proper image of might and

---

[114] 'One of the *oldest* records'—though probably of the age of David, not of Deborah: see note [82] and *App.*III.

[115] It *may* have been—but I see no reason whatever for concluding that it actually *was*—an *Israelitish* symbol. It may just as well have been a *Canaanitish* symbol, and been adopted by the Hebrews with the worship of the tribes around them.

majesty[116]; hence a prince is called the steer of his people, D.xxxiii.17,* [*comp.* Ps.lxviii.30.] Perhaps, we may compare the form of Moloch with a steer's head, or Melkarth, and Astarte riding on a steer, the myth of Europa and the steer, that of the Minotaur, &c. But it would be folly to maintain withal that Israel derived this symbol from Phœnicia or elsewhere.[117] On religious ground Israel had originality enough to think out this for itself. How little progress an anti-national religion made in Israel, Ahab found with his Baal-worship.[118]

122. Thus in the gold gazelles we find no signs of JHVH-worship at Mecca. Are there also plain evidences that *another* Deity was worshipped? Prof. Dozy attempts to show that the Simeonites brought with them a *Saturn*-worship; and he dwells upon the fact that Mahommedans, living in the twelfth

---

[116] It may not be easy to show why a *heifer*, as we suppose, rather than a *steer*, as Dr. Oort thinks, was chosen as a symbol of the Baal. But, of neat cattle, according to the Arabians, Dozy *p.*88, the *female* is superior; of small cattle the *male*; and so in the Bible, the 'heifer' is taken as an example of vigorous strength, Jer.xlvi.20,xlviii.34,l.11, Hos.x.11, quite as often as the 'steer,' Jer.xxxi.18, xlvi.21, Mal.iv.2, and, in fact, (107*), the heifer is almost always spoken of as 'used for ploughing or threshing.' May this be one reason why the 'heifer' was specially chosen as a symbol of the *Sun*, from its connection with the labours of the field, upon which the blessing of that Deity was especially sought? In D.xxxiii.17, to which Dr. Oort refers, quite a different formula is used —'the first-born of his ox.'

[117] I would not 'maintain' this: but it seems to me highly probable that the Israelites, together with the worship of the Sun-Deity, borrowed also the symbol of the heifer from the Syro-Phœnician tribes. The examples which Dr. Oort has produced, especially that of the 'Tyrian Baal,' Melkarth, a figure of a man with the head of a steer [? heifer], tend to confirm this.

[118] The state of Israel at its first entrance into Canaan, when, as we suppose, it adopted the religion of the tribes of the land, as we are told it did, Ju.ii.12,13,17, &c., was totally different from its advanced condition at the time when Ahab attempted to substitute the worship of the Tyrian Baal for that of JHVH, the Syrian Baal; for this latter had been now practised for centuries among them, and had long been recognised as the *national* form of religion.

---

* Princes are compared elsewhere to 'he-goats,' Is.xiv.9. A representation of JHVH under the form of a he-goat is, therefore, not in itself inconceivable. But there is no proof that this symbol was ever employed.—OORT.

century after Christ, knew very well that the Meccan territory was dedicated to Saturn, *p.*85.

123. I willingly allow that they followed in this a true tradition, and that the orthodox adherents of Mahommed were much in the wrong to be offended with this. The fact, that Saturn or Kronos was worshipped in Arabia, is established by a much older witness, *viz.* NONNUS (IV Cent.), who says of Hercules (*Dionys.* xl.369, &c., quoted by Mov. i.*p.*182,183),—

He is named on the Euphrates *Belus*, in Lybia *Ammon*, *Apis* on the Nile, the *Kronos* of Arabia, the Assyrian *Zeus*.

Thus, in the fourth century after Christ, a Saturn-worship was spread in Arabia.

124. That Hobal represented this Deity is very probable. It was a figure of an old man;[119] and Saturn was also imagined elsewhere under this form. Mov.i.*p.*287,288. But what does this prove for the worship of the first Israelitish colonists? Absolutely nothing. If it could be shown that the image of Hobal was as old as this, and that it was always regarded as an image of Saturn, then the matter would have been raised beyond doubt. But the contrary may be demonstrated from the writings of Prof. DOZY himself.

125. The Arabians, indeed, themselves say that their Hobal had come from elsewhere, and that the prince Hamr-Ibn-Lokhei brought it from Mesopotamia or Moab to Mecca. Prof. DOZY rejects these accounts because they conflict with each other, and because no people will allow such a novelty to be forced upon them. But who tells us that the inhabitants of this

---

[119] This figure of the 'old man' *may*, perhaps, have been substituted, in course of time, for the original image of the Simeonites (? a *heifer*), long, perhaps, decayed by time or destroyed by violence. But 'the Baal' was probably represented in Israel by a *human* figure, as well as under the form of a heifer: *comp.* Ez.xvi.17,—' Thou didst take also thy fair jewels of my gold and of my silver, which I had given thee, and madest to thyself *images of man*, and didst commit whoredom with them, and tookest thy broidered garments and coveredst them; and thou didst set mine oil and mine incense before them.'

district adopted this chief Deity *merely* upon the authority of their prince? Connected by commercial transactions with Syria or Mesopotamia, the Arabian tribes about Mecca, if they did not themselves possess a definite religion, might at any time have adopted Deities and forms of worship from one of these regions. There were 360 idols in the Temple of Mecca; so that novelties were introduced to superfluity.[120]

126. The fact, which Prof. Dozy mentions, *p.*203, *viz.* that the descendants of the 'Gorhum'—[*i.e.* the *second* set of Israelitish emigrants (1), who settled at Mecca during the Babylonish Captivity,]—were driven from the holy soil, because they resisted the introduction of novelties, shows us that the Chozaha did not leave altogether unchanged the religion which they found at Mecca.[121] Mahommed, who had the image destroyed without hesitation, as soon as he became master of Mecca, seems therefore not to have regarded it as a part of the primitive religion which he desired to restore.[122]

127. But there is a stronger proof that the image of Hobal dates from a considerably later time. When, for instance, the

---

[120] But these were not the '*chief* Deity' at Mecca. Admitting, as Dr. OORT does, that the Simeonites *did* found the Sanctuary at Mecca, did they leave behind *no* definite religion? It is easy to account for the introduction of numerous idols—though 360 is probably an exaggeration—when the Simeonite traditions about 'the Baal' had long passed away, or become very faint. But the '*chief* Deity' would surely not be likely to have been introduced in this way.

The tradition, therefore, that Hobal came from Mesopotamia or Moab, seems to point rather to the Israelitish origin, supposed by Prof. Dozy. And even if the *image* 'Hobal' was of more recent origin, yet the *name* = hab-Baal, 'the Baal,' may have been handed down from ancient times as the name of the Great Deity: and this, in fact, Dr. OORT allows to be conceivable (128) and probable (132,133).

[121] But they found *a* religion of some kind at Mecca; and there is no reason to suppose that they abolished it *altogether*, and introduced their 'novelties' in such a way, as to get rid of the very name of the chief Deity who had been hitherto worshipped there.

[122] This argument seems inconclusive. In the same way we might maintain that the primitive religion of Israel contained no idolatries, because the Prophets *assume* this. Mahommed had learned to abhor all images, and *therefore* he destroyed Hobal.

Chozaha expelled the Jewish settlers in Mecca, these latter buried the two golden gazelles and breastplates. But why did they not bury also the image of Hobal, if it already existed? *That* was, of course, the most sacred thing of all. When the treasures were again dug up, the image was in the Temple; for lots were cast for them in front of it. Hence it was probably placed there in the interval of time between the burying of these sacred objects, and their being dug up again.[123]

128. But, even if the image was of a later age, the 'well' itself at Mecca may have dated from the days of the Simeonites, and the ancient name Hobal may have been merely applied to the image in later days. Does this name denote 'the Baal'? Much may be brought against this conjecture, however simple it seems. That 'Baal' is abridged into 'Bal,' presents no difficulty. But the vowel *o* is not so easy to be explained. Prof. Dozy shows that *a* can be interchanged with *o*: but that is not the only question here. Baal with the article forms not *habaal* but *hab-baal*; and it is strange that the double *b* does not appear.[124]

129. The greatest difficulty, however, lies precisely in the use of the article itself. That the Israelites, among whom we find the worship of many 'Baalim,' named the Tyrian Baal *par excellence* 'the Baal,' is self-evident. It is natural also that

---

[123] But much, surely, would depend upon the *size* of Hobal, upon its *form* and *construction*, upon the *material* of which it was composed. The *golden gazelles* and the (probably *gilt*) *breastplates* and *swords*, were, no doubt, valuable articles, and they were small and handy, so as to be easily buried. But, if Hobal was merely a heavy figure of agate-stone, in the form of a man, Dozy, *p.*82, with no gold ornamentation or artistic skill bestowed upon it, they may not have *cared*, or may not have *been able*, to bury it. The very fact, that they buried such easily portable articles as the swords and breastplates, shows that they did this in haste, or under difficulties. A stone image might be easily replaced: not so golden gazelles.

[124] Dr. Oort says himself (118) that '*vowels* are usually modified when a word passes from one language to another.' Why, then, if the Simeonites said *hab-Baal* or *hab-Bal*, may not the *tribes about Mecca* have said hob-Bal or even (with one *b*) *Hobal*?

'to burn incense to the Baal' became a general designation for all idolatrous and unlawful worship.[125] But, supposing that there ever was in ancient times a worshipping of a Deity 'Baal,' certainly his worshippers did not name him with the article; for this is not used before Proper Names.[126]

130. Appeal may be made to the generality of meaning of the word 'Baal,' *viz.* 'Lord.' But *Adonis* denotes the same; and yet this divine name has passed over to the Greeks, not in the form *ha-Adon*, 'the Lord,' but as a Proper Name without the article.[127] Whoever finds with me in 'Baal' nothing but a general designation of the Deity, may maintain that the article should be placed before it, whenever there is no closer definition of it, as 'of the well,' 'of Judah,' &c. But the name which the territory of the Simeonites in Arabia bore anciently, 'Gedor-Baal,' that of their town in Canaan, 'Baal,' and that of 'Kirjath-Baal,'—all without closer definition, and yet without an article—show that in the name 'Hobal' also we must not look for any article.[128]

[125b] But see note [105], in opposition to this view.

[126] Quite true: Baal was *not* a Proper Name: and our translation is faulty in not having everywhere 'the Baal' for 'Baal.' In like manner 'Lady' or 'Virgin' cannot be used for 'Mary': it must be always 'our Lady,' 'the (our) Lady of, &c.,' 'the Virgin,'—(see the Lectionary of the Church of England, under the 'Lessons Proper for Holy Days,' where we have still retained a remnant or 'rag' of Romanism, *viz. Annunciation of our Lady.*') And so it was always 'the Baal'=the Lord, 'our (their) Baal,' 'the Baal of,' &c. On our view, therefore, this supposed objection becomes a strong argument in favour of Prof. Dozy's view that Hobal really means 'the Baal.' It is certain that the Israelites *did* worship some Baal *before* the Tyrian Baal was introduced among them, as appears from the names 'Eshbaal,' &c. And what Baal would this have been but 'the Lord,' the Sun, Adonis, JHVH, the 'God of the land'?

[127] The Greeks may, perhaps, have taken over, in 'Adonis,' the form אֲדֹנִי, *Adoni*, 'my Lord,' not הָאָדוֹן, *ha-Adon*, 'the Lord.' But, in fact, the LXX have used 'Baal' without the article, in 1K.xviii.21, 2Ch.xxiii.17,17. We are speaking here, however, of the people about Mecca,—not of the Greeks. If civilised men dropped the article in adopting the name *ha-Adon*, that is no reason why rude barbarians should have been so discriminating. If the Simeonites spoke to them of *habbal*, what wonder is it if they regarded it as the Proper Name of the Deity, and called it Hobal?

[128] How do they show this? Why should not the image of 'the Baal' have

131. There is not the least reason for stopping to consider why the religion of the expatriated Simeonites should not have been JHVH-worship.[129] The names of several of their leaders compounded with the name JHVH, 1Ch.iv.34–37, point to this, as Prof. Dozy also has remarked, *p*.100.[130] This is further supported by the fact of their giving to their new abode the name 'Shiloh,' *p*.97, inasmuch as in the place of that name in Canaan stood the great Sanctuary of JHVH, to which frequent pilgrimages were made.

132. Can any other evidence be produced for this? An idea has occurred to me, which I entertain with great hesitation, because I feel on how weak a foundation it rests. It is this. The name 'Hobal' is probably very old. Certainly, until the middle of the fifth century after Christ descendants of Israelites were guardians of the Meccan sanctuary, *p*.204,205. The Choza*h*a, who had possession of the supreme power, had made many innovations there in the worship, *p*.203, to the great disgust of the zealous Gorhum. Among other things, as said above, they had introduced the image of Hobal[?] and others. But it is not probable that if the name of the chief Deity was changed, Jews would either be still found willing to undertake the office or be endured as guardians.

133. Thus the name Hobal [that is, as Dr. Oort here supposes, the name of the chief *Deity* himself, previously and still worshipped at Mecca,—not of the *image*, which he supposes

---

been called Hobal = 'the Baal,' though the Israelites might speak of 'Gedor-Baal,' 'Kirjath-Baal,' &c., just as now we speak of Kings-Town, Queen-Street, Lady-Day, &c.?

[129] This is true in the sense of their worshipping JHVH as 'the Baal' of Canaan; and they *may* have known his mysterious name, JHVH, and, of course, they *did* know it, if the names of their leaders, 1Ch.iv.34–37, are genuine, many of them being compounded with JHVH; and that such names might exist in that age we know from those of the sons of Samuel, Saul, and David, some of which are Jehovistic. But, if they did, they have left behind no other trace of their having known it.

[130] They migrated early in David's reign: and nearly a century before this time Samuel had called his sons by names compounded with JHVH, 1S.viii.2.

to have been made afterwards, and merely called by his name,] will have been no longer understood. Is it possible that the name JHVH may lie hid in it? We no longer know with certainty how this name was pronounced. But in Proper Names we have constantly יהו, *Jahu*, *e.g.* in Jerem*jahu* =Jeremiah, &c: and I see no reason why that should be an abbreviation. From *Jahu* is to be explained the form of the name at the beginning of Proper Names, *Jeho* or *Jo*, as in *Jeho*shua, *Jo*el. Also, if we write the name JHVH, as is now generally done, as the imperfect of הוה, *viz. Jahveh*, we shall have the sound *Jahwe* or *Jahuë*, if the *v* is not pronounced sharply.

134. If this is true, then it is not impossible that the ancient name of the Meccan deity was at full length *Jahuë, Baal of Ishmael*, or something of that kind—perhaps, *Jahuë, Baal of the Well*; but this last I would not contend for, because it is uncertain whether, under the title 'Baal of the Well' and similar names, JHVH himself was worshipped anciently in Israel, or rather, perhaps, a subordinate Deity.* It is a common occurrence that in course of time the *Ja* or *Je* should be dropped,—*e.g. Khizkiyyah* (Hezekiah)=*Jekhizkiyyah*—[and so there would arise *huë-baal*=*Hobal.*¹³¹]

135. Meanwhile, whether the above conjecture be accepted or not, it does not decide the main question. In any case JHVH ¹³² was the God of the Simeonites; and there is no evi-

---

¹³¹ It appears to me that this derivation, however ingenious, is far more improbable than that supposed by Prof. Dozy. But Dr. OORT allows that 'Baal' is *part* of the word. Then, surely, 'hab-Baal' must have been the whole of it.

¹³² Rather, 'in any case the Baal of Syria,—whose mysterious name, whether known to them, or not, or, rather, whether *used* by them familiarly, or not, at the time of their expatriation, was JHVH,—was the God of the Simeonites.'

---

* If in 'Gedor-Baal' JHVH himself was worshipped, does not this support the view, which I have advanced with hesitation in § 2, that originally JHVH, and no subordinate Deity, was worshipped in the Sanctuaries, 'Baal of Judah,' &c.? OORT. [Certainly: but whether *everywhere* and *in all ages* the Syrian Baal was worshipped in Israel under the *name* JHVH, is not so certain : see note ¹³⁹.—*Ed.*]

dence to show that they worshipped him under any one visible form or another. We have not learned anything new from the Meccan Sanctuary as to the relation between JHVH and the Baalim.[133] In this matter, even after Prof. Dozy's admirable discovery, the O.T. remains still our only help. Is anything more to be expected from Mecca, having reference, in this or in any other respect, to the ancient religion of Israel?

136. We know now that the pre-Islamite religion of the Arabians was partly derived from Israel. The decyphering of the great Festival of Islam,—' a *tableau vivant* of the Feast on the Gilgal,' (as my friend Dr. DE GOEJE names it, in his notice of Prof. Dozy's work, *Gids* for May, 1864, *p*.297–312,)—and many other particulars, give us good hope that the cultivators of Arabian Literature will, with further study, bring us much more light upon the subject. And certainly I can reckon upon the assent of all who are interested in the study of the antiquities of Israel, when I conclude with the assurance that we shall be grateful to Prof. DOZY, as well as to all his fellow-students in the same department of Science, if out of Mecca they shall be able to dissipate somewhat of the obscurity, in which the ancient condition of Israel is still to a great extent hidden.

[133] *If* the name JHVH was known to the Simeonites ([131]), as the names in 1Ch.iv.34-37, if genuine, would imply,—and *if* the name of the Chief Deity at Mecca was anciently ([132]), in the Simeonitish time, *Hobal*,—and *if* this name means really, as we suppose, *hab-Baal*,—then we have learned from the Meccan Temple this fact, that JHVH was most probably regarded popularly by the Jews of David's time as identical with 'the Baal.' This is no *new* fact, it is true; for it is also indicated, as we have seen, in the Bible. And it throws no more light on 'the relation of JHVH to the Baalim': but it leaves them still, as we have found them to be, in all probability, only representatives of 'the Baal' at different localities in Israel.

APPENDIX I.

ANALYSIS OF E.XX.1-17.

(i) *v.*2, the phrase, 'brought thee out of the land of Egypt,' occurs identically in D.v.6,vi.12,viii.14,xiii.10(11), and *nowhere else in the Bible*; though other varieties of this formula, *e.g.* 'brought you, them, us, Israel, &c. out of Egypt,' occur repeatedly in Deuteronomy and elsewhere: see (*P.V.Anal.*79.ix).

(ii) *v.*2, 'house of servants,' D.v.6,vi.12,vii.8,viii.14,xiii.5(6),10(11),—*nowhere else in the Bible*, except Jer.xxxiv.13.

(iii) *v.*3, 'other gods,' D.v.7,vi.14,vii.4,viii.19,xi.16,28,xiii.2,6,13,xvii.3,xviii.20, xxviii.14,36,64,xxix.26,xxx.17,xxxi.18,20, and also E.xxiii.13,* xxxiv.14.*

(iv) *v.*4, בֶּסֶל, *pesel*, 'graven-image,' D.iv.16,23,25, v.8, xxvii.15, and also L.xxvi.1,*—*nowhere else in the Pentateuch*.

(v) *v.*4, תְּמוּנָה, *těmunah*, 'likeness,' D.iv.12,15,16,23,25,v.8, and also N.xii.8.|

(vi) *v.*5, 'bow down and serve,' D.iv.19,v.9,viii.19,xi.16,xvii.3,xxix.26(25) xxx.17, and also E.xxiii.24,*—*nowhere else in the Pentateuch*.

(vii) *v.*5, קַנָּא, *kanna*, 'jealous,' D.iv.24,v.9,vi.15, and also E.xxxiv.14,* comp. D.xxix.20(19),xxxii.16,21.

(viii) *v.*5, 'visiting the iniquity of the fathers upon the children, unto the third and fourth generation,' as in E.xxxiv.7.*

(ix) *v.*6, 'doing mercy to thousands,' *comp.* E.xxxiv.7,* 'keeping mercy to thousands.'

(x) *v.*6, 'keep my commandments,' D.iv.2,40, v.10,29, vi.2,17, vii.9,11, viii.2,6,11, x.13, xi.1,8,22, xiii.4,18, xix.9, xxvi.17,18, xxvii.1, xxviii.9,45, xxx.10,16, G.xxvi.5, (*P.V.Anal.*164), and also E.xvi.28, L.xxii.31, xxvi.3.*

(xi) *v.*7, לֹא יְנַקֶּה, *lo yěnakkeh*, 'will not clear,' D.v.11, and also E.xxxiv.7,* N.xiv.18,*—*nowhere else in the Pentateuch*.

(xii) *v.*8, זָכוֹר, *zachor*, 'remember,' D.xxiv.9, xxv.17, and also E.xiii.3*; comp. D.ix.7,27, xxxii.7, and also E.xxxii.13.

(xiii) *v.*10, 'thy stranger that is within thy gates,' D.v.14, xiv.21, xxxi.12; *comp.* also 'the Levite that is within thy gates,' D.xii.12,18, xiv.27, xvi.11; and note that *neither of the above formulæ occurs elsewhere in the Bible*: so 'thy gates' occurs

---

* All these passages I believe to be Deuteronomistic. But I have not space here to show this, or to enter into the questions which arise out of this analysis. It is sufficient at present to notice that the phrases in question,—if used at all by *other* writers of the Pentateuch,—are clearly *most common and familiar* with the Deuteronomist.

29 times in Deuteronomy, but *nowhere else in the Pentateuch*, and *only besides in very late passages, viz.* Ps.cxxii.2, cxlvii.13, Is.liv.12, lx.11,18, Ez.xxvi.10.

(xiv) v.12, 'that thy days may be long in the land,' D.v.16, *comp.* 'that thou mayest prolong thy days in the land,' D.iv.40, v.33, xxx.18, xxxii.47, *comp.* also D.iv.1, vi.2, viii.1, xi.21, xvi.20, xxx.6,15–20, and also E.xxiii.26.*

(xv) v.12, 'the ground which Jehovah thy Elohim giveth thee,' repeated identically in D.iv.40, v.16, xxi.1,23, xxv.15,—*nowhere else in the Bible*; *comp.* also the similar phrases, 'the land which Jehovah thy Elohim giveth thee,' D.iv.21, xv.4.7, xvi.20, xvii.14, xviii.9, xix.2,10,14, xxiv.4, xxv.19, xxvi.1,2, xxvii.2,3, xxviii.8,—'thy gates which Jehovah thy Elohim giveth thee,' D.xvi.5,18, xvii.2,—'the nations whose land Jehovah thy Elohim giveth thee,' D.xix.1,—'these peoples whom Jehovah thy Elohim giveth thee,' D.vii.16, xx.16,—with other variations, *viz.* 'the mountain of the Amorites (land, inheritance, cities,) which Jehovah (our (your) Elohim, the Elohim of your fathers) giveth us (them,)' D.i.20,25, ii.29,iii.20, iv.1, xi.17,31, xii.9, xiii.12, Jo.i.11,15 (P.V.5)—*not one of which formulæ occurs anywhere else in the whole Bible.*

From the above analysis it seems almost certain that the first edition of the Decalogue, in E.xx, is due to the Deuteronomist, as well as the second in D.v. Consequently, the repeated use of the phrase 'Jehovah thy Elohim,' in E.xx.2,5, 7,10,12, is only an instance of the Deuteronomistic peculiarity, noticed in *P.*III.554.

On the *traditionary* view, we should have to suppose that Moses having made use of the phrases (i), (ii), (xiii), (xv), in the record of the solemn utterance of the Ten Commandments, in the *third month* of the Exodus, never used any one of them again in any of his writings until his last address in the *fortieth* year, and then began suddenly to use each one of them freely. The same remark applies also to (iii), (vi), (xiv), whether, or not, we take into account the fact that E.xxiii.20–33, xxxiii.12–xxxiv.28, appear to be Deuteronomistic interpolations; since these passages belong to the same period in the story as the utterance of the Ten Commandments.

APPENDIX II.

THE DEUTERONOMISTIC ORIGIN OF N.X.33–36.

In N.x.33 we have the expression 'Ark of the Covenant of Jehovah,' a phrase which is used repeatedly by the *Deuteronomist*, x.8,xxxi.9,25,26, Jo.iii.3,17,iv.7,18, vi.8,viii.33, *comp.* also 'Ark of the Covenant,' Jo.iii.6,6,8,11,14,iv.9,vi.6,—'Ark of Jehovah,' Jo.iii.13,iv.5,11,vi.11,12,vii.6—*all*, most probably, Deuteronomistic passages; and not one of these formulæ occurs anywhere else in the Pentateuch, except the first of them in N.xiv.44.

But N.xiv.40–45, also, is evidently Deuteronomistic; see D.i.41–43, and *comp.*

---

* See note, p.79.

especially the expression 'be smitten before those hating you,' N.xiv.42, with similar expressions occurring *only* (in the Pentateuch) in D.i.42,xxviii.7,25, and L.xxvi.17.

And L.xxvi, again, is, as we believe, a Deuteronomistic insertion; and at all events it is pronounced by KUENEN, *Eng. Ed. p.*207, to be of *later* origin than L.xviii-xx, while these three chapters are, according to him, *p.*71, 'in their present form *younger than Solomon*,' and, according to OORT, *het Menschenoffer in Israel, p.*123, 'transfer us into *the very same age as Deuteronomy.*'

Thus the formula in question, with its kindred formulæ, appears to be in every instance the special property of the Deuteronomist.

On the other hand, in the other portions of the Pentateuch we have always 'Ark of the Testimony,' E.xxv.22,xxvi.33,34,xxx.6,26,xxxi.7,xxxix.35,xl.3,5,21, N.iv.5, vii.89, Jo.iv.16ᵇ; *comp.* also 'Tabernacle of the Testimony,' E.xxxviii.21, N.i.50, 53,53,ix.15,x.11,xvii.7,8,xviii.2, 'Vail of the Testimony,' L.xxiv.3,—not one of which phrases is used by the Deuteronomist.

Hence it seems that N.x.33-36 is of Deuteronomistic origin, a conclusion confirmed by the fact that in N.x.35 we have the Pihel form מְשַׂנְאֶיךָ, 'those hating thee,' as in D.xxxii.41, xxxiii.11, *nowhere else in the Pentateuch*; and in N.x.36 רְבָבָה, 'ten thousand,' as in D.xxxii.30, xxxiii.2,17, and only twice besides in the Pentateuch, *viz.* G.xxiv.60, which we have shown to be (probably) Deuteronomistic (*P.V.Anal.*145), and L.xxvi.8, also, apparently, due to the same writer.

APPENDIX III.

THE LATER ORIGIN OF THE SONG OF DEBORAH, JU.V.1-31.

The following are the arguments which seem to us decisive *against* placing the date of the origin of this Song in the time of the Judges.

(i) There are no genuine poems of any length in the Bible,—no elaborate highly-finished compositions like this,—which date from an earlier age than that of David. The poems in Genesis are all due to the Jehovist of David's time, (see note [27]); the Mosaic origin of the Hymn of Moses, E.xv.1-18, is admitted by Prof. KUENEN to be doubtful (see also note [27]); the prophecies of Balaam, from the reference to David himself and his conquests in N.xxiv.17-19, cannot date from an earlier time than that of David; the 'Song of Moses,' D.xxxii.1-43, and the 'Blessing of Moses,' D.xxxiii.1-29, belong to the still later age of the Deuteronomist. Thus we have nothing comparable to the 'Song of Deborah' in the Mosaic age, nor any poem besides whatever, that is even ascribed to the time of the Judges—except the 'Song of Hannah,' 1S.ii.1-10, which is manifestly a Psalm of a later time, that has been adapted to her case, though very clumsily,—see especially *v.*10, 'He shall give strength unto His king, and exalt the horn of His anointed,' which could have had no meaning in her days. But, if such a splendid poem as the 'Song of Deborah' was really composed in the very midst of the time of the Judges, and has been handed down to us in so complete and accurate a form, it would seem very strange and almost inconceivable that no traces of any other similar composition, by the same or some other writer, should have been preserved in the traditions of the people.

(ii) The fact that this Song is said to have been sung by Deborah *and* Barak, *v.*1, militates at once against the notion of its genuineness. For how can we conceive *Barak* to have taken any part in singing it?

(iii) Some expressions of the Song are identical with those of Ps.lxviii, as shown by the italics below.

Ju.v.	Ps.LXVIII.
*v.*3, To JHVH I will *sing*, I will *sing-praise* to JHVH.	*v.*4, *Sing* to Elohim, *sing-praise* to His Name.
*v.*4, JHVH, *in Thy going forth* from Seir, *In Thy marching* from the field of Edom, *The earth trembled, the heavens* also *dropped,* The clouds also dropped water.	*v.*7, Elohim, *in Thy going-forth*, before Thy people, *In Thy marching* in the wilderness, *v.*8, *The earth trembled, the heavens* too *dropped,*
*v.*5, *Before* JHVH the mountains melted, *That Sinai before* JHVH, *the Elohim of Israel.*	*Before* Elohim, *That Sinai before* Elohim, *the Elohim of Israel.*
*v.*12, *Lead-captive Thy captivity.*	*v.*18, *Thou leddest-captive captivity.*

It seems certain from the above that either the Psalmist had before him the Song of Deborah, or the writer of the Song had before him the words of the Psalm. And, that the latter was most probably the case, is seen from the fact that the 'Elohim' of the Psalm is everywhere changed to 'JHVH' in the Song: for it is far more likely that a later writer should change 'Elohim' into 'JHVH,' than that the Psalmist should have changed 'JHVH,' the name of the covenant-God of Israel, into 'Elohim'—nay, should have changed 'JHVH, the Elohim of Israel,' into 'Elohim, the Elohim of Israel.'

Besides which, *v.*7,8, of the Psalm are manifestly part of the context. On the other hand, in the Song there is an appearance of an *expansion* of the words of the Psalm: thus the expressions 'from Seir,' 'from the field of Edom,' of the Song, seem equivalent to the simple phrase, 'in the wilderness,' of the Psalmist, and the additional statements, 'the clouds also dropped water,' 'the mountains melted,' are merely *amplifications* of the words of the Psalm, and the first of them rather a superfluous tautology.

We conclude, therefore, that the Song was written *after* the Psalm,—that is, after the twelfth year of David's reign, *P.V.*213.*

(iv) The fact that no reproach is thrown on *Judah,* as on Reuben, Gilead, Dan, and Asher, for not taking part in this war with the Canaanites, may be explained, perhaps, by this circumstance, that the writer lived under David, and under the sovereignty of the tribe of Judah. It can hardly be sufficiently explained by the *distance* of Judah from the scene of conflict, or even from this tribe being closely occupied with the Philistines (*P.V.*190); since Reuben was, surely, equally removed, and doubtless had also its fears from hostile neighbours as well as Judah.

---

* This agrees, of course, with the view expressed in *P.V.App.*II.49–52, as to the later origin of the name JHVH, and its gradual introduction into the religious history of Israel, and tends to support that view, but is itself altogether independent of it.

Simeon also is not named, either as being almost absorbed in Judah, or as being insignificant in numbers in the writer's time: see *P.V.App.*I.

(v) The fact that the tribe of *Levi* is not mentioned, and that not a word is put into the mouth of the Prophetess having reference to the *Priesthood, Ark*, or *Tabernacle*, seems to be decisive against the historical truth of the story in the Pentateuch. At the time when this Song was written, it is plain, the Levites could not have filled any important office in Israel. Hence it was most probably composed at some time during the reign of David, before the Temple was built, and the Priesthood had gained a more dignified position.

(vi) The language in *v*.8, 'Was there a shield or spear seen among forty thousand in Israel?' seems to refer to the early times of Saul and Samuel, 1S.xiii.19–22, of which a lively tradition was still retained in the age of David. And the expression in *v*.10, 'Ye that ride on white asses,' suits the same time, as asses or mules were used by chief persons, 1S.xxv.20, 2S.xvi.2, xvii.23, xix.26, 2S.xiii.29, 1K.i.33,38,44, down to the time of Solomon, when *horses* seem to have been first used commonly in Israel, 1K.x.26,28,29.

APPENDIX IV.

THE COMPOSITE CHARACTER OF THE STORY OF GIDEON, JU.VI–IX.

(i) In ix Gideon is *always* called *Jerubbaal, v*.1,2,5,5,16,19,24,28,57, of which *v*.24,57, may be by the Compiler; whereas in vi,vii,viii, we have *always* 'Gideon,' (*eleven* times,) except in vi.32, where the name Jerubbaal is derived; and so in vii,viii, *after* this giving of the surname, he is still called 'Gideon' *always* (*twenty-eight* times), except in vii.1, 'Jerubbaal, who is Gideon,' viii.35, 'the house of Jerubbaal-Gideon,' and viii.29, where Jerubbaal occurs simply, as in ix,—'and Jerubbaal, the son of Joash, went and dwelt in his own house.' It seems likely, therefore, that ix, for the most part, and probably also viii.29, are from one author, and vi,vii,viii, for the most part, from another, or, at least, from one writing at another time.

(ii) The above conclusion is confirmed by finding that in ix 'Elohim' is *always* used as the Personal Name for the Deity, *v*.7,9,13,23,56,57, (*v*.57, perhaps, as before, by the Compiler), *never* 'Jehovah': whereas in vi,vii,viii, 'Jehovah' is used *forty* times, and 'Elohim,' as a Personal Name, only in vi.36,39,40, vii.14, viii.3, (though it occurs also as an appellative, 'Jehovah, the Elohim of Israel,' vi.8, 'Jehovah your (thy, their) Elohim,' vi.10,26, viii.34, 'angel of Elohim,' vi.20,) and of these five instances two, vii.14, viii.3, occur in a formula, which was almost proverbial (see *P.V.p*.194, note), 'Elohim gave.'

It would seem as if vi.36–40, and perhaps vii.1, introducing Gideon's surname 'Jerubbaal,' may be part of the same document as ix, and the rest of vi,vii,viii, for the most part, may be the product of another hand or of another age. This would explain also why Gideon, after the appearance of the angel of Jehovah in vi.11–24, still doubts and requires a sign in *v*.36–40.

APPENDIX IV.

(iii) Prof. KUENEN observes, i.*p*.210—'vi–viii exhibits so great an agreement with the Jehovistic passages of the Pentateuch, that STÄHELIN has been able to suppose that the Jehovist is the author of these chapters. This inference may go too far: it is noticeable that the agreement in question is *wholly wanting in* ix. This fact also leads us to ascribe to that chapter a different origin from the foregoing.'

But *is* the agreement in question wholly wanting in ix? *Comp*.ix.2, 'I am your bone and your flesh,' with G.xxix.14, 'Surely thou art my bone and my flesh'; and *comp.* also ix.3, 'for they said, He is our brother,' *v*.18, 'for he is your brother,' with G.xxix.15, 'for that thou art my brother.' May not Ju.ix really be, as STÄHELIN supposes, due to the Jehovist, as well as Ju.vi–viii, but have been written at an earlier period than the main portions of the latter chapters—written, for instance, about the time, in the early or middle part of David's life, in which the second set of Jehovistic insertions in Genesis (J^2) were written (see *P.V.*287), to which G.xxix belongs, and in which he has used 'Elohim' very predominantly, or written at a yet earlier time, in the reign of Saul, when (J^1) was composed, in which he has used 'Elohim,' as here, exclusively?

But, however this may be, it is plain that the story of Gideon is a *composite* account, due either to different authors, or to the same author writing at different times: and vi.25–32 belongs apparently to the *later* set of insertions. If these, in accordance with our conjecture above, were written by the Jehovist at a later part of his career, *e.g.* in the latter part of David's reign, it is possible that in that age he may have already come to dislike the use of the name 'Baal,' inasmuch as the worship of the Baal (JHVH) in various parts of the land conflicted greatly with the effort to establish a purer worship of Jehovah on Mount Zion. It may be, therefore, that what did not offend him thirty or forty years before, when he wrote the original story of Jerubbaal,—at a time when Saul, Jonathan, and David, in the presence of Samuel and his followers, could call their sons without compunction by the name of the Baal,—was no longer tolerable. Hence, in rewriting a portion of the narrative, he may have sought to explain away the meaning of the name Jerubbaal, as expressing Gideon's devotion to the Baal, by making it arise out of an act of his, which was intended to put down the worship of the Baal and establish that of Jehovah.

This would agree with the fact that *after* David's time we do not find any of the kings of Judah or Israel—even the worst kings—calling their sons by the name of the Baal. It is supported also by the circumstance, mentioned already, as proving the dislike of the Prophets of David's age and afterwards for the name 'Baal,' that in no single psalm or prophecy, except Hos.ii.16, is 'Baal' used as a synonym for Jehovah. Dr. OORT's view of the substitution of 'Jerubbesheth' for 'Jerubbaal' in 2S.xi.21, as being intended to *suppress* the fact of his name having been originally compounded with 'Baal,' seems hardly tenable. For how could this unpleasant fact have been concealed, if they wrote (with Dr. OORT) '*Shame*-defender' for '*Baal*-defender,' or rather, as we suppose, 'Shame-strives' for 'Baal-strives'? And the same remark applies to the change of Eshbaal, Meribbaal, and Baalyadah, into Ishbosheth, Mephibosheth, and Elyadah. Clearly, in the case of the first two of these the change was made from a desire to *censure*, not to *conceal*, the fact in question, which the substituted 'Bosheth' would immediately betray,— 'the Bosheth' being actually used for 'the Baal' in Jer.iii.24, xi.13, Hos.ix.10;

APPENDIX IV.   85

comp. ἡ αἰσχύνη of the LXX, 1K.xviii.19,25, Jer.iii.24, Hos.ix.10, while in Jer.xi.13 they represent 'the Bosheth' of the Heb. Text by ἡ Βάαλ. From the above it might even be supposed that the changes in question might have been made as early as the time of the Deuteronomist. But we must here draw attention to the following phenomenon.

In the LXX version of 2S.v.14–16 we have the names of *twenty-four* sons of David, 'born to him in Jerusalem,' and among these are Ἐλιδαέ = *Elyadah*, and Βααλιμάθ, compounded with Baal. But on examination it will be seen that this list is in reality only a *double* list of nearly the same twelve names, some of them strangely corrupted. The Heb. Text of the same passage has only *eleven* names; but in 1Ch.xiv.4–7 it has *thirteen*, which appear also in the LXX; and the LXX list of twenty-four names in 2S.v.14–16 is formed by the combination of these two lists of *eleven* and *thirteen*, as appears below.

	2S.v.14–16.			1Ch.xiv.4–7.	
Heb.	LXX.		Heb.	LXX	
Shammuah	Σαμμούς	Σαμαέ	Shammuah	Σαμαά	
Shobab	Σωβάβ	Ἰεσσιβάθ	Shobab	Σωβάβ	
Nathan	Ναθάν	Ναθάν	Nathan	Ναθάν	
Solomon	Σαλωμών	Γαλαμαάν	Solomon	Σαλωμών	
Ibkhar	Ἐβεάρ	Ἰεβαάρ	Ibkhar	Βαάρ	
Elishuah	Ἐλισουέ	Θησοῦς	Elishuah	Ἐλισά	
	Ἐλιφαλάτ		Elpalet	Ἐλιφαλήθ	
	Ναγέδ		Nogah	Ναγέθ	
Nepheg	Ναφέκ	Ναφέκ	Nepheg	Ναφάθ	
Japhiah	Ἰεφιές	Ἰωνάθαν	Japhiah	Ἰαφιέ	
Elishamah	Ἐλισαμά	Λεασαμύς	Elishamah	Ἐλισαμαέ	
Elyadah	Ἐλιδαέ	Βααλιμάθ	Baalyadah	Ἐλιαδέ	
Eliphalet	Ἐλιφαλάθ	Ἐλιφαάθ	Eliphalet	Ἐλιφαλά.	

Thus Βααλιμάθ is evidently no *new* name compounded with Baal, but only a corruption of Baalyadah.

Now, it is mainained by Prof. Dozy that 'Baalyadah' was changed by the later Scribes into 'Elyadah' in 2S.v.16, but left standing in 1Ch.xiv.7, because the Books of Samuel were much more generally read than the Books of Chronicles (Dozy, *p*.38). And this seems to be confirmed by the following facts. In the LXX version of 2S.v.14–16, we find Ἐλιδαέ and Βααλιμάθ, that is, manifestly, *both* Elyadah and Baalyadah: so that the LXX translators found, probably, Elyadah in one copy of Samuel and Baalyadah in another. But the LXX has 'Jerubbaal' in 2S.xi.21 as well as in 1S.xii.11,—showing, apparently, that 'Jerubbaal' was the original reading in *both* passages, and that the change into 'Jerubbesheth' had been made in the Heb. Text of 2S.xi.21 at so late a time, that it had not found its way into the MSS. which the Greek translators used. There can be little doubt, therefore, that these alterations were made, as Prof. Dozy after Geiger supposes, by Jewish Scribes *after the Captivity.*

APPENDIX V.

THE COMPOSITION OF HEBREW NAMES WITH THE DIVINE NAME.

1. The following synopsis of the different modes, in which Hebrew Names are compounded with the Divine Name, may be useful to students, and may help also to throw some light upon the religious condition of Israel.

2. Compounds with *El*:—
    (i) *prefixed*, as *El*kanah, *El*iphaz, &c.;
    (ii) *affixed*, as Isra*el*, Adbe*el*, &c.:
N.B. Kabzeel, Jo.xv.21, = Jĕkabzeel, Neh.xi.25, &c.

    Compounds with *Jehovah* or *Jah*:—
    (i) *prefixed*, as *Jo*chebed, *Jeho*ash, &c.;
    (ii) *affixed*, as Amar*iah*, Amaz*iah*, &c.:
N.B. Azaniah, Neh.x.9, = Jaazaniah, Jer.xxxv.3, &c.

3. Different forms of the same name, with *El* or *Jah* interchanged:—

*El*iyakim	*Jeho*yakim		
*El*ishaphat	*Jeho*shaphat		
*El*zaphan			Zephan*iah*
*El*iphelet			Pelat*iah*
*El*ihud			Hod*iyah*
	Jĕkhezk*el* (Ezekiel)		Jĕkhizk*iyyah* (Hezekiah)
	Zadk*iel*		Zedek*iah*
	Bĕthu*el*		Bith*iah*
	Haza*el*		Haza*iah*
		*Jeho*ahaz	Ahaz*iah*
*El*ishama	Ishma*el*		Ishma*iah*
*El*asah	As*iel*		Asa*iah*
*El*zabad	Zabd*iel*	*Jeho*zabad	Zebad*iah*
*El*iada	Yĕdiă*el*	*Jeho*iada	Yeda*iah*
*El*nathan	Nĕthan*el*	*Jeho*nathan	Nĕthan*iah*
*El*hanan	Hănan*el*	*Jeho*hanan	Hanan*iah*
*El*iezer	Azar*el*, Azri*el*	*Jo*ezer	Azar*iah*

4. Names compounded with both *El* and *Jah*:
*El*i-*yah* or *El*i-*jah*, *Jo-el*, *El-jo*-enai, 1Ch.vii.8, comp. *El*ienai, viii.20.

5. Other words are used similarly in Proper Names to express the Deity, as בַּעַל, *Baal*, 'Lord,' מֶלֶךְ, *Melech*, 'King,' אָדוֹן, *Adon*, 'Lord,' צוּר, *Tsur*, 'Rock' or 'Stone,' אוּר, *Ur*, 'Fire.'

APPENDIX V.

*Baal*yah, *Malch*iyah, *Adon*iyah, *Uri*yah, comp. *El*iyah;
*Baali*ada, comp. *El*iada, *Jeh*oiada;
*Baalh*anan, comp. *Elh*anan, *Jeh*ohanan;
Jerub*baal*, comp. *Jeh*oyarib; so Hanni*bal* (Phœnician)=Hanni*el*.

N.B. Ash*bel*, G.xlvi.21, probably=Esh*baal*, comp. *Esh-Jehovah*, 'Fire of Jehovah,' N.xi.1,3, *Esh-Elohim*, 'Fire of Elohim,' 2K.i.12;
*Malch*iel, *Zur*iel, *Ur*iel, comp. *El*iel, Joel;
*Malch*izedek, *Adon*izedek, comp. *Jeh*ozadak;
*Malch*ishua, comp. *El*ishua, *Jeh*oshua;
*Malch*iram, *Adon*iram, comp. *Jeh*oram.

N.B. *Had*oram, 2Ch.x.18,=*Ad*oram, 1K.xii.18,=*Ad*oniram, 1K.iv.6,v.14, comp. *Jeh*oram. Also *Had*oram, son of Toi, 1Ch.xviii.10,=*J*oram, 2S.viii.10; where we note (i) the real identity of *J*oram and *Ad*oniram, and (ii) the fact that the son of the *Syrian* king Toi has a name '*J*oram' compounded with *Jehovah* or JHVH.

Elim*elech*, Eli*zur*, comp. Eli*el*, Eli*yah*;
Nathan*melech*, comp. Něthan*el*, Nethan*iah*;
Ebed*melech*, comp. Abdi*el*, Obad*iah*;
Tob*adon-iah*, comp. Tob*iah*, Tab*el*;
*Zur*ishaddai, comp. *El*shaddai;
Pedah*zur*, comp. Pedah*el*, Pedah*iah*.

So Beth-*Zur*, Jo.xv.58, the name of a place, may be compared with Beth-*El*, Beth-*Dagon*, Beth-*Baal*, Beth-*Peor*, Beth-*Shemesh*.

N.B. In 1Ch.ix.36 we find mentioned as brothers of Ner, Saul's grandfather, both *Baal* and *Zur*.

6. That צוּר, 'Rock,' was used in Israel, as a name for the Deity, is plain from the following instances.

'the Rock (LXX, Θεός), His work is perfect.' D.xxxii.4.
'the Rock (LXX, Θεόν), who begat thee, thou neglectest.' v.18.
'except their Rock (LXX, ὁ Θεός), had sold them.' v.30.
'for their Rock (οἱ θεοὶ αὐτῶν) is not as our Rock (ὁ Θεὸς ἡμῶν).' v.31.
'and he shall say, Where is their Elohim,
their Rock, in whom they trusted?' v.37.
'there is no Rock like our Elohim.' 1S.ii.2, comp. 2S.xxii.32, Ps.xviii.31.
'my Elohim, my Rock in whom I trust.' 2S.xxii.3, Ps.xviii.2.
'blessed be my Rock!' 2S.xxii.47, Ps.xviii.46, cxliv.1.
'to me said the Rock of Israel.' 2S.xxiii.3.
'Jehovah, my Rock.' Ps.xix.14, xxviii.1.
'my Rock (ὁ Θεός μου), be not thou silent unto me.' Ps.xxviii.1.
'He only is my Rock,' Ps.lxii.2,6.
'they remembered that Elohim was their Rock.' Ps.lxxviii.35.
'my Rock (ὁ Θεός μου), and there is no unrighteousness in Him.' Ps.xcii.15.
'by Jah-Jehovah is the Rock of everlasting ages.' Is.xxvi.4.
'unto the Rock (πρὸς τὸν Θεόν) of Israel.' Is.xxx.29.
'Is there an Eloah beside me?
There is no Rock (Θεός): I know not any.' Is.xliv.8.
'Jehovah! Thou hast ordained them for judgment,
And Rock! for correction hast thou founded them.' Hab.i.12.

7. There are no similar instances of אוּר, 'Fire,' being used as the Divine Name, the nearest approach to it being in Is.xxxi.9, 'Jehovah, whose *Fire* is in Zion': and though Jehovah is twice compared to a *Light* (אוֹר), Ps.xxvii.1, Mic.vii.8, and He is once spoken of as 'the Light of Israel,' Is x.17, yet these examples are not like those which are quoted above in the case of 'Zur'; and besides, in the names *U*riel, *U*rijah, the word compounded is *U*r, 'Fire,' not *O*r, 'Light.' Hence it might be supposed that in the above names *U*r is not used as a Personal Name for the Deity, but only as an appellative—'Fire of El,' 'Fire of Jah.' But in Shed*eu*r (שְׁדֵיאוּר) we have *U*r also inserted at the *end* of a name, which seems to imply that it was used as a Personal Name, whatever may be the meaning of the other part of the word, שְׁדֵי. If this is equivalent to שַׁדַּי, 'Shaddai,' then we should here have two Divine Names joined in one word, as in Eli-el, Eli-jah, Jo-el, Baal-jah, Eli-zur, and Zuri-shaddai.

8. But אֵשׁ, 'Fire,' is frequently used as a symbol of Jehovah's presence, *comp.* G.xv.17, E.iii.2,2, xix.18, xxiv.17, D.iv.36, v.25, xviii.16, Is.xlvii.14, Lam.ii.3, Ez.i.27, viii.2, Mal.iii.2, and especially the following passages :

'Jehovah thy Elohim is a Devouring Fire,' D.iv.24 ;
'Jehovah thy Elohim, He it is that passeth-over before thee ;
Devouring Fire, He shall destroy them,' D.ix.3 ;
'Who among us shall sojourn with the Devouring Fire ?
Who among us shall sojourn with the Eternal Burnings ?' Is.xxxiii.14.

N.B. The above words are usually supposed to refer to the flames of Hell. But in reality they have nothing to do with Hell-Fire. On the contrary, in this passage the expressions 'Devouring Fire,' 'Eternal Burnings,' are evidently merely synonyms for the Deity ; for the answer to the question, 'Who shall sojourn with the Devouring Fire ?' is given immediately, 'He that walketh righteously, and speaketh uprightly; he that despiseth the gain of deceits, that shaketh his hands from holding a bribe, that stoppeth his ears from hearing of blood, and shutteth his eyes from seeing evil ; he shall dwell on high ; his place of defence shall be the munitions of rocks ; bread shall be given him ; his water shall be sure. Thine eyes shall see the King in His beauty ; they shall behold the land that is very far off.' *v.*15-17.

Comp. Ps.xv throughout, which indeed is almost an exact counterpart of this passage :

'Jehovah, who shall sojourn in Thy Tabernacle ?
Who shall dwell in Thy holy hill ?
He that walketh uprightly, and worketh righteousness, and speaketh the truth in his heart,' &c., and 'taketh not a bribe against the innocent.
He that doeth these things shall never be moved.'

9. It is scarcely necessary to show that 'Jehovah' was called מֶלֶךְ, 'King,' in Israel : *comp.* the passage just quoted, Is.xxxiii.17, also 1S.xii.12, Ps.v.2, x.16, xxiv.7,8,9,10, xxix.10, xliv.4,xlvii.2,6,7,xlviii.2,lxviii.24, lxxiv.12,lxxxiv.3, lxxxix.18, xcv.3, xcviii.6, cxlv.1, cxlix.2, Is.vi.5, &c. Jer.xlviii.15.

That He was also called אָדוֹן or אֲדוֹנָי is notorious ; and it is plain from the above Proper Names, as well as from Hos.ii.16, that He was called 'Baal.'

10. But, besides the above, it would seem that אָב, *Ab*, 'Father,' אָח, *Akh*,

APPENDIX V.

'Brother,' עָם, Ham (E.V. *Am*), 'People,' אֶבֶן, *Eben*, 'Stone,' עֵזֶר, *Ezer*, 'Help,' הוֹד, (הָדָר) הֶדֶר, (הֲדַד) הָדָד, אֲדָד, *Hod*, *Hadar*(*Hadad*), *Heder*(*Eder*), 'Splendour, glory,' שֵׁם, *Shem*, 'Name,' are also used in Proper Names as synonyms for the Deity.

Akh-ab (Ahab), *comp. Jo-el, Eli-jah, Eli-zur*, &c.
*Ab*iel, *Amm*iel, *Az*riel, *Shem*uel, *comp. El*iel, Joel, *Malch*iel, *Zur*iel, Uriel.
Eliab, *Eliam*, *comp. Eliel*, *Elijah*, *Elimelech*, *Elizur*.
*Ab*ijah, *Akh*ijah, *Hod*ijah, *comp. El*ijah, *Baal*jah, *Malch*ijah, *Adon*ijah, *Ur*ijah.
*Ab*ihu, *comp. El*ihu.
*Ab*ihud, *Akh*ihud, *Amm*ihud, *comp. El*ihud.
*Ab*itub, *Akh*itub, *comp. Tabel, Tobiyah, Tobadoniyah.*
*Ab*ida, *Shem*ida, *comp. El*iada, *Jeh*oiada, *Baal*iada.
*Ab*imelech, *Akh*imelech, *Ad*rammelech, *comp. El*imelech.
*Ab*inadab, *Akh*inadab, *Amm*inadab, *comp. Jeh*onadab.
*Ab*ner, *Ab*iner, *comp.* Neriyah.
*Ab*ram, *Ab*iram, *Akh*iram, *Am*ram, *Shem*iramoth, *comp. Jeh*oram, *Malch*iram, *Adon*iram.

N.B. Probably, Hiram (חִירָם) = Akhiram (אֲחִירָם), as אֲרָמִים = רָמִים, 2Ch.xxii.5. So we have *Beth-haRam*, 'House of the High-One,' Jo.xiii.27, *comp. Beth-El*, &c.
*Ab*iezer, *Akh*iezer, *Eb*enezer, *Had*arezer, *Shem*ezer, *comp. El*iezer, *Jo*ezer.
*Akh*ikam, *Azr*ikam, *comp. Adon*ikam.
*Jarob*am (Jeroboam), *comp. Jeh*ojarib, *Jerub*baal.
*Rekhab*eam (Rehoboam), *comp.* Rekhabiah.
*Jashob*am, *comp.* Shebuel, Shobiah.
*Amm*ishaddai, *comp. Zur*ishaddai.
*Amm*izabad, *comp. El*zabad, *Jeh*ozabad.

N.B. In 1Ch.ix.36 we find mentioned among the brothers of Ner, Saul's grandfather, both *Ner* and *Zabad*, which are used above in the composition of names.

11. That *Ab*, 'Father,' is used in the foregoing as a synonym for the Deity, is apparently shown by the fact of our finding both *Abiel* and *Eliab*, in which the words *Ab* and *El* are clearly put *in apposition*, = 'Father-God' or 'God-Father,' not *in construction*, = 'Father of God' or 'God of Father.'

And there is no doubt that Jehovah is spoken of in the Bible as 'Father'; *comp.* Ps.lxviii.5,lxxxix.26, and especially the following passages:

'Thou art our Father . . . Thou, Jehovah, art our Father.' Is.lxiii.16.
'Now, Jehovah, Thou art our Father.' Is.lxiv.8.
'Saying to a stock, [instead of to Jehovah,] Thou art my Father,
And to a stone, Thou hast begotten me.' Jer.ii.27.
'Wilt thou not from this time cry unto me,
My Father, Thou art the guide of my youth?' Jer.iii.4.
'I said, Thou shalt call me, My Father,
And shalt not turn-aside from after Me.' Jer.iii.19.
'For I am a Father to Israel.' Jer.xxxi.9.
'If then I be a Father, where is mine honour?' Mal.i.6.
'Have we not all one Father? Hath not one God created us?' Mal.ii.10.

Hence we have *Ab* plainly used as equivalent to *El* in *Abi-hu*, 'the Father is He,'=*Eli-hu*, 'El is He,' comp. D.xxxii.39, *Ani-hu*, 'I am He,' which indicates its meaning in all the other instances, as *Abimelech* = *Elimelech*, *Abner* (Father-Lamp) =*Nerijah* (Lamp-Jah), comp. *Eli*-hu, 1Ch.xxvii.18, =*Eli-ab*, 1S.xvi.6, 1Ch.ii.13.

In fact, *Ab-ram*, 'High-Father,' was one of the names of the chief Deity, the Sun, Adonis, JHVH, at Byblus, *P.V. App*.III.12. Comp. also the Phœnician Divine Name, אָב אַדִּיר, 'Mighty Father,' Dozy, *p*.24, and observe that in 1S.iv.8 we have '*Mighty* ELOHIM,' in Is.xxxiii.21, '*Mighty* Jehovah.' Is it possible that the idea of using the name 'Abram,' as that of the ancestor of Israel, may have arisen from this employment of the name in the worship of the Phœnician Deity?

12. It is not so easy to show that the other words quoted in (10) were freely used in speaking of the Deity. But, certainly, אֲחִיָּה, *Akhijah*, must mean either 'Brother of Jah' or 'Brother-Jah'=Jah is a Brother. The former of these being, of course, out of the question, we are thrown back upon the latter, and can only regard 'Brother' as a name applied to the Deity,—probably in the sense of 'confederate, friend,'=the *covenant*-God of Israel, comp. Am.i.9, 'they (the Tyrians) remembered not the *covenant of brethren* (with Israel),' and so Hiram calls Solomon 'my brother,' 1K.ix.13.

Hence the meaning of *Akhimelech* must probably be explained, not 'brother of the king,' but 'Brother-King,' comp. *Elimelech*, and so in other instances.

13. Still more singular is the use of עַם, 'People,' to represent the Deity. Yet, if *Ammiel* might be explained to mean 'People of El,' what can *Eliam* mean but 'El-People'? In short, *Ammiel, Eliam*, correspond exactly to *Zuriel, Elizur*, as these also do to *Joel, Elijah*. So *Ammihud*, 'People-Splendour,'=*Elihud*, 'El-Splendour,' *Abihud*, 'Father-Splendour,' *Akhihud*, 'Brother-Splendour.' And, just as we have *Jehoram* (Jehovah is High), *Malchiram* (the King is High), *Adoniram* (the Lord is High), we have also *Abiram* (the Father is High), *Akhiram* (the Brother is High), *Amram* (the People is High). So, again, *Ammishaddai* (the People is Almighty) = *Zurishaddai* (the Rock is Almighty),—*Ammizabad* (the People gave) = *Elzabad, Jehozabad*,—*Amminadab* (the People gave-freely) =*Jehonadab, Abinadab, Akhinadab*.

And once more יָרָבְעָם, *Jarob-am*, which some explain as meaning 'the people are many,' seems rather to mean 'the People strives,' comp. יְרֻבַּעַל = יָרֻב בַּעַל, *Jarub-baal*, 'the Baal strives,' יְהוֹיָרִיב, *Jehojarib*, 'Jehovah strives'; and רְחַבְעָם, *Rĕkhab-am*, corresponds to רְחַבְיָה, *Rĕkhab-iah*, meaning 'the People (Jehovah) is (wide, large, spacious=) grand or great.'

14. Upon the whole it seems scarcely possible to doubt that the word עַם, 'People,' is used in Proper Names to express the Deity. May it be because the People was so closely identified with its Deity? Comp. the following passages:

'Chemosh shall go forth into captivity.' Jer.xlviii.7.

'Woe be unto thee, O Moab! the people of Chemosh perished,' *v*.46.

'Bel boweth down, Nebo stoopeth.' Is.xlvi.1.

'Babylon is taken, Bel is confounded, Merodach is smashed.' Jer.l.2.

'I will punish Bel in Babylon, &c.' Jer.li.44.

APPENDIX V.

May it be, in short, that as the Father is one with His children, so the Covenant-God of Israel was regarded as one with His people? Jehovah was 'with them,' 'in the midst of them,' 'subduing the people under them, and the nations under their feet,' 'choosing their inheritance for them, the excellency of Jacob whom He loved,' &c., Ps.xlvi-xlviii. Hence, in E.xvii.16, N.xxi.14, Ju.v.23,31,—that is, in *David's* days, when, as we suppose (notes [28,31,32]), these passages were written, the wars of Israel are styled the wars of JHVH,—the inhabitants of Meroz are cursed, because they 'came not to the help of JHVH,'—the enemies of Israel are the enemies of JHVH,—in short, JHVH seems to have been identified with Israel.

15. It is noticeable that *all* the names in the Bible, which are compounded thus with עם, belong to the age of *David*, 2S.iii.5, ix.4,5, xiii.37, xvii.27, 1Ch.iii.3,5, xi.11, xii.6, xxvii.2, xv.10,11, xxvi.5, xxvii.6, 1K.xi.26,&c. 2Ch.ix.29,&c. 1K.xi.43, &c. 1Ch.iii.10, 2Ch.ix.31,&c.—(at least, Rehoboam was born in David's life-time, *comp.* 1K.xi.42, xiv.21, and Jeroboam was probably about the same age,)—or they occur only in those parts of the Pentateuch and Ruth, which were probably written in the age of *David*, E.vi.18,20,23, N.i.7,10,12, ii.3,18,25, iii.19,27, vii.12, 17,48,53,66,71, x.14,22,25, xiii.12, xxvi.58,59, xxxiv.20,28, R.iv.19,20,—or else they are found in passages of the Chronicles which refer to these, 1Ch.ii.10, vi.2,3,18, xxiii.12, xxiv.20, xxvi.23,—with, however, the following exceptions,—

Jeroboam II, King of *Israel*, 2K.xiii.13, xiv.16,&c. 1Ch.v.17,&c. Hos.i.1, Am.i.1, vii.9,10,11, —

1Ch.vi.22, where *Korah* appears as the son of *Amminadab*, the son of *Kohath*, where, however, *Amminabad* is obviously a mistake for *Izhar*, as the margin of the E.V. corrects it, *comp. v.*18, where the sons of Kohath are given, *Amram*, *Izhar*, *Hebron*, *Uzziel*, as in E.vi.18, and *v.*37,38, where *Korah* is given as the son of *Izhar* the son of *Kohath*,—

1Ch.vii.26, where *Ammihud* is given in the very doubtful genealogy of Joshua (*P.*I.111-113):—

1Ch.ix.4, where another *Ammihud* appears, seemingly in the reign of *David*, see *v.*2,3,22,38,39, though the whole passage is very obscure (*P.*II.232):—

Ezr.x.34, where *Amram* occurs in a list of names after the Captivity.

16. Except, therefore, in the last instance, where the name may have been copied from the Amram of the Pentateuch,—and in that of Jeroboam II, where the name may have been taken from that of his great ancestor,—we have no distinct instance of a single name compounded with עם, except in the reign of *David*, when the idea of the *Nation*, as in covenant with God, was most fresh and lively. At all events, we have no instance of a *new* name of this kind, formed after the Davidic age. See (51) and note [31].

17. Again, אבן, 'Stone,' seems, like צור, 'Rock,' to be also used for the Deity in G.xlix.24, 'from thence is the Shepherd, the *Stone* of Israel,' and, therefore, perhaps also in the name *Ebenezer* = *Eliezer*, *Joezer*, *Abiezer*, *Akhiezer*. It is true, a different explanation of this name is given in 1S.vii.12, as if it meant merely 'stone of help,' with reference to a memorial-stone then erected by Samuel, who said, 'Hitherto hath Jehovah helped us.' But it is possible that this may be only a later attempt to explain a name which already existed, 1S.iv.1,v.1, (though in

APPENDIX V.

these passages the name *may* be used proleptically,) and that, in fact, it was the name of this *sacred* stone, before the time of Samuel.

18. Also עֶזֶר, 'Help,' appears in *Eliezer, Joezer, Azriel*, comp. *Elizur, Zuriel*; and see E.xviii.4, D.xxxiii.7,29, Ps.xxxiii.20, lxx.5(6), cxv.9,(10),11, cxlvi.5, Hos.xiii.9.

So הוֹד, &c. 'Glory,' in *Elihud, Hodiyah*, comp. *Eliel, Eliyah*; and see Job xxxvii.22, Ps.xxi.5,(6), xcvi.6, cxlv.5, cxlviii.13, Is.xxxv.2, &c.

And שֵׁם, 'Name,' in *Shemuel, Shemezer, Shemida, Shemiramoth*, comp. *Eliel, Joezer, Eliada, Jehoram*; and see E.iii.15, vi.3, xv.3, xxiii.21, Ps.lxviii.4(5), &c.

19. It is remarkable that several of the above words, used to express the Deity, are used also, uncompounded, as the names of men; though Dozy, *p.*82 note, says, 'No man bears the name of a Deity.' Thus we have—

Baal, 1Ch.viii,30; *Melech*, 1Ch.viii.35, ix.41;
Zur, N.xxv.15, xxxi.8, 1Ch.viii.30, ix.36;
Ur, 1Ch.xi.35, *comp. Uri*, E.xxxi.2, 1K.iv.19, Ezr.x.24;
Abi, 2K.xviii.2;
Akhi, 1Ch.v.15, vii.34, *comp. Ekhi*, G.xlvi.21, =*Akhiram*, N.xxvi.38,
Ezer, 1Ch.iv.4, vii.21, xii.9, Neh.iii.19, xii.42;
Hod, 1Ch.vii.37, *Hadad*, 1K.xi.14,17, &c.

20. Dozy, *p.*22,31, connects the use of 'Rock,' 'Stone,' as names for the Deity, with the worship of JHVH, whose emblem was often a large stone or mass of rock. There may be some ground for this. And it is certainly possible that the idea of using 'Devouring Fire' as a symbol for Jehovah may have originated from the use of this emblem in Sun-worship. But most of the above names seem to be used merely in a metaphorical sense, to express the attributes of the Deity, *e.g.* 'Lord,' 'Father, 'Brother,' 'Help,' 'Glory,' 'Name,' and, apparently, 'People.'

21. Dozy notes as follows, *p.*30. 'Among the old proper names, which often afford a rich source of information as to the modes of thought of a people, we find *Elizur, Zuriel, Zurishaddai*. Not that men will have actually borne these names: it would be absurd to maintain this; they are names out of the half-mythical age, and appear only in Numbers.' But see 1Ch.ix.36, where *Baal* and *Zur* are both given as names of the brothers of Ner, Saul's grandfather. It rather appears to me, as observed in (15, 16), that such names as these belong mostly to the age of David.

22. GEIGER, in his *Urschrift*, &c., in which he describes at length the corruptions of the original Hebrew Text of the Bible, which have been made by the later Jews for religious or other reasons, has some remarks upon the substitution of הַשֵּׁם, 'the Name,' for 'Jehovah,' which we give here somewhat abridged, as follows: *p.*261-274.

'When the faith in the One Spiritual God, laboriously acquired, had become at length the innermost property and withal the distinguishing characteristic of Judaism, strenuous efforts had to be made to express this also distinctly in the collection of ancient records, and every apparently unconformable expression had to be removed, or at all events altered. Very special attention would be given, of course, to the name of God, which belonged exclusively to Judaism, the name יהוה. All other designations for the Deity express simply some kind of relation, in which

God stands to the world and to mankind; or they describe Him with reference to some inherent property,—*e.g.* overpowering Might, Lord, King, Father, Merciful, &c. *This* Name only was believed to express the full nature of God, to represent Him according to His absolute Eternity, His inexhaustible Fullness, and His exalted Majesty, as El Elyon. This Name, then, must be treated exactly in the same way as God Himself: the Majesty of God must also be reverenced in the Name peculiar to Him: that name also was unapproachable, *unutterable*. Hence in all passages, where it occurred in the Scriptures, it must be replaced for public reading by other expressions.

'The Greek Translators did this by actually rendering it by one of the other Divine Names, the holiest in some sense next to the Tetragrammaton, and like it quadriliteral, *viz.* אֲדֹנָי, Κύριος. This, however, did not apply in Palestine, since in the original tongue the name Adonai also might not be lightly uttered, where it did not exist in the Text; and besides, by this substitution for the unutterable Name of another Name also of frequent occurrence, no indication would be given that in these places *that* Name stood originally, and was only replaced by another. Hence a better contrivance was to substitute for it הַשֵּׁם: 'the Name' was an innocent formula, and yet it expressed plainly that here the real Proper Name of God was intended, only was not to be uttered. This is what the Samaritans did who read it thus in the Pentateuch, and wrote it thus in their later writings. But so also did the Jews of Palestine. They employed this circumlocution not only in common life, when they wished to express the Divine Name emphatically, as in the expressions קְדֻשַּׁת הַשֵּׁם, 'hallowing of the Name,' חִלּוּל הַשֵּׁם, 'desecration of the Name,' but also when they wished expressly to utter the Tetragrammaton, even when quoting Biblical expressions, and actual verses of the Bible which were meant to be uttered.

'With this accords the old tradition that with the death of Simon the Just the Priests ceased to use 'the Name' in the Priestly Blessing. This tradition means evidently that after his time the use of the Tetragrammaton was discontinued even by the Priests, nay, by the High-Priest, and that, too, on the Day of Atonement in his most solemn duties. This tradition, which has maintained itself in spite of the manifest contradiction which it presents to later statements, involves certainly an historical fact, *viz.* this, that in ancient times the utterance of the Divine Name was dropped even in the holiest ceremonies. This old tradition seems to have been reproduced also in the view of Abba Saul, who said that, whoever uttered 'the Name' according to its letters, would have no part in the life to come. But this view did not prevail generally in later times, since this saying is indicated with others as an addition of an individual. Rather, the Halachah assumes that the High-Priest actually expressed the Tetragrammaton, by remarking that the Priests and People, so soon as they heard the 'express Name' (שֵׁם הַמְפוֹרָשׁ) uttered, fell down on the ground; and the embellishing legend declares that the voice of the High-Priest, when he uttered 'the Name' on the Day of Atonement, was heard as far as Jericho. And not by the High-Priest only, on the Day of Atonement, was 'the Name' to be outspoken; but the Priests, generally, in the daily Priestly Blessing, N.vi.23-26, uttered 'the Name' in the Temple 'according to its written form, expressly,' (שֵׁם הַמְפוֹרָשׁ כִּכְתָבוֹ). Nay, the Pharisees went yet further. They ordered, in opposition to the 'heretics,' *i.e.* the Samaritans and Sadducees, that in the usual greeting 'the Name' should be used, and it is added: 'Formerly, when the doctrine of the Lord was forgotten in Israel, the Scribes swallowed-up the Name,' *i.e.* they so connected it with other words of the sentence, that it could not be distinctly caught with the ear; and precisely against this practice was the later Pharisaic ordinance directed.

'Thus the Halachah recognises the use of the Tetragrammaton in common life, and blames only the misuse of it. Afterwards the dread for the utterance of the holy Name returned. It was maintained that, whereas formerly *in* the Temple the High-Priest and the Priests generally in the Priestly Blessing, uttered this peculiar Name, yet *outside* the Temple they pronounced, and were obliged to pronounce, the Blessing with a circumlocution. It is only in later times that we find the distinct notice, that יהוה indeed was written, but אדני was read. And now first the practice was adopted, which the Alexandrians had already of old introduced into their translation, but which certainly did not penetrate earlier into Palestine for the original Hebrew. Through the Masoretic pointing, which followed, no doubt, an usage already established, it first became general to read everywhere אדני where יהוה stood in the Hebrew.

'In L. xxiv. 10-16 we have the story of the man, who, born of an Israelite and an Egyptian mother, uttered blasphemies against God; and the legislative direction is thereupon given that such an offender should be stoned. Here the blasphemies are of the most determined kind, expressed by the word נקב, and they are especially so, inasmuch as God is named in them with the Tetragrammaton. It is the most flagrant kind of blasphemy that could be uttered, and must be so represented to the hearer. Here there was only one resource,—that with which we started at the beginning of this enquiry. What was done generally with reference to the utterance of the Divine Name, was applied here also to the Text. For the Divine Name הַשֵּׁם was substituted: this expression, which of itself said nothing Divine, yet in the most distinct manner indicated the Tetragrammaton. In making this change, however, they went to work with great delicacy. In the principal clause, at the beginning of *v.* 16, they left the Divine Name standing, but they inserted שֵׁם between it and נָקַב. On the other hand, in the narrative, *v.* 11, and in the recapitulation, *v.* 16, which establishes for all without exception the law already laid down, they omitted the Proper Name of God, and replaced it by הַשֵּׁם (which the *Sam.* reads also in *v.* 16) or שֵׁם, as we read in the latter instance. These readings were manifestly not the original ones. It is quite contrary to Biblical usage to put הַשֵּׁם absolutely for God,—still more, to put שֵׁם without the article, which is, in fact, ungrammatical, and can only have been inserted thus purposely in this correction, with the view of pointing attention to it. Also, נָקַב or קבב is never used with שֵׁם, unless the person blasphemed is mentioned, as is the case at the beginning of *v.* 16.'

May not the use of שֵׁם, *Shem*, as a name for the Deity, in such names as *Shem*uel (Samuel), *Shem*ida, *Shem*iramoth, *Shem*ezer, throw light upon these phenomena?

39 Paternoster Row, E.C.
London, *July* 1865.

GENERAL LIST OF WORKS,

NEW BOOKS AND NEW EDITIONS,

PUBLISHED BY

Messrs. LONGMANS, GREEN, READER, and DYER.

Arts, Manufactures, &c.	11
Astronomy, Meteorology, Popular Geography, &c.	7
Biography and Memoirs	3
Chemistry, Medicine, Surgery, and the Allied Sciences	9
Commerce, Navigation, and Mercantile Affairs	18
Criticism, Philology, &c.	4
Fine Arts and Illustrated Editions	10
General and School Atlases	19
Historical Works	1
Index	21—24
Knowledge for the Young	20
Miscellaneous and Popular Metaphysical Works	6
Natural History and Popular Science	8
Periodical Publications	20
Poetry and the Drama	17
Religious Works	12
Rural Sports, &c.	17
Travels, Voyages, &c.	15
Works of Fiction	16
Works of Utility and General Information	18

Historical Works.

The History of England from the Fall of Wolsey to the Death of Elizabeth. By JAMES ANTHONY FROUDE, M.A. late Fellow of Exeter College, Oxford.

Vols. I. to IV. the Reign of Henry VIII. Third Edition, 54s.

Vols. V. and VI. the Reigns of Edward VI. and Mary. Second Edition, 28s.

Vols. VII. and VIII. the Reign of Elizabeth, Vols. I. and II. Third Edition, 28s.

The History of England from the Accession of James II. By Lord MACAULAY. Three Editions, as follows.

LIBRARY EDITION, 5 vols. 8vo. £4.

CABINET EDITION, 8 vols. post 8vo. 48s.

PEOPLE'S EDITION, 4 vols. crown 8vo. 16s.

Revolutions in English History. By ROBERT VAUGHAN, D.D. 3 vols. 8vo. 45s.

Vol. I. Revolutions of Race, 15s.

Vol. II. Revolutions in Religion, 15s.

Vol. III. Revolutions in Government, 15s.

An Essay on the History of the English Government and Constitution, from the Reign of Henry VII. to the Present Time. By JOHN EARL RUSSELL. Third Edition, revised, with New Introduction. Crown 8vo. 6s.

The History of England during the Reign of George the Third. By WILLIAM MASSEY, M.P. 4 vols. 8vo. 48s.

The Constitutional History of England, since the Accession of George III. 1760—1860. By THOMAS ERSKINE MAY, C.B. Second Edition. 2 vols. 8vo. 33s.

Historical Studies. I. On some of the Precursors of the French Revolution; II. Studies from the History of the Seventeenth Century; III. Leisure Hours of a Tourist. By HERMAN MERIVALE, M.A. 8vo. 12s. 6d.

Lectures on the History of England. By WILLIAM LONGMAN. Vol. I. from the Earliest Times to the Death of King Edward II. with 6 Maps, a coloured Plate, and 53 Woodcuts. 8vo. 15s.

A Chronicle of England, from B.C. 55 to A.D. 1485; written and illustrated by J. E. DOYLE. With 81 Designs engraved on Wood and printed in Colours by E. Evans. 4to. 42s.

History of Civilization. By HENRY THOMAS BUCKLE. 2 vols. £1 17s.

    VOL. I. *England and France*, Fourth Edition, 21s.

    VOL. II. *Spain and Scotland*, Second Edition, 16s.

Democracy in America. By ALEXIS DE TOCQUEVILLE. Translated by HENRY REEVE, with an Introductory Notice by the Translator. 2 vols. 8vo. 21s.

The Spanish Conquest in America, and its Relation to the History of Slavery and to the Government of Colonies. By ARTHUR HELPS. 4 vols. 8vo. £3. VOLS. I. & II. 28s. VOLS. III. & IV. 16s. each.

History of the Reformation in Europe in the Time of Calvin. By J. H. MERLE D'AUBIGNÉ, D.D. VOLS. I. and II. 8vo. 28s. and VOL. III. 12s.

Library History of France, in 5 vols. 8vo. By EYRE EVANS CROWE. VOL. I. 14s. VOL. II. 15s. VOL. III. 18s. VOL. IV. nearly ready.

Lectures on the History of France. By the late Sir JAMES STEPHEN, LL.D. 2 vols. 8vo. 24s.

The History of Greece. By C. THIRLWALL, D.D. Lord Bishop of St. David's. 8 vols. 8vo. £3; or in 8 vols. fcp. 28s.

The Tale of the Great Persian War, from the Histories of Herodotus. By GEORGE W. COX, M.A. late Scholar of Trin. Coll. Oxon. Fcp. 7s. 6d.

Ancient History of Egypt, As- syria, and Babylonia. By the Author of 'Amy Herbert.' Fcp. 8vo. 6s.

Critical History of the Lan- guage and Literature of Ancient Greece. By WILLIAM MURE, of Caldwell. 5 vols. 8vo. £3 9s.

History of the Literature of Ancient Greece. By Professor K. O. MÜLLER. Translated by the Right Hon. Sir GEORGE CORNEWALL LEWIS, Bart. and by J. W. DONALDSON, D.D. 3 vols. 8vo. 36s.

History of the Romans under the Empire. By CHARLES MERIVALE, B.D. Chaplain to the Speaker.

    CABINET EDITION, 8 vols. post 8vo. 48s.

    LIBRARY EDITION, 7 vols. 8vo. £5. 11s.

The Fall of the Roman Re- public: a Short History of the Last Century of the Commonwealth. By the same Author. 12mo. 7s. 6d.

The Conversion of the Roman Empire: the Boyle Lectures for the year 1864, delivered at the Chapel Royal, Whitehall. By the same. 2nd Edition. 8vo. 8s. 6d.

Critical and Historical Essays contributed to the *Edinburgh Review*. By the Right Hon. Lord MACAULAY.

    LIBRARY EDITION, 3 vols. 8vo. 36s.

    TRAVELLER'S EDITION, in 1 vol. 21s.

    In POCKET VOLUMES, 3 vols. fcp. 21s.

    PEOPLE'S EDITION, 2 vols. crown 8vo. 8s.

Historical and Philosophical Essays. By NASSAU W. SENIOR. 2 vols. post 8vo. 16s.

History of the Rise and Influence of the Spirit of Rationalism in Europe. By W. E. H. LECKY, M.A. Second Edition. 2 vols. 8vo. 25s.

The Biographical History of Philosophy, from its Origin in Greece to the Present Day. By GEORGE HENRY LEWES. Revised and enlarged Edition. 8vo. 16s.

History of the Inductive Sciences. By WILLIAM WHEWELL, D.D. F.R.S. Master of Trin. Coll. Cantab. Third Edition. 3 vols. crown 8vo. 24s.

Egypt's Place in Universal His- tory; an Historical Investigation. By C. C. J. BUNSEN, D.D. Translated by C. H. COTTRELL, M.A. With many Illustrations. 4 vols. 8vo. £5 8s. VOL. V. is nearly ready, completing the work.

Maunder's Historical Treasury; comprising a General Introductory Outline of Universal History, and a Series of Separate Histories. Fcp. 10s.

Historical and Chronological En- cyclopædia, presenting in a brief and convenient form Chronological Notices of all the Great Events of Universal History. By B. B. WOODWARD, F.S.A. Librarian to the Queen. [*In the press.*

History of the Christian Church, from the Ascension of Christ to the Conversion of Constantine. By E. BURTON, D.D. late Regius Prof. of Divinity in the University of Oxford. Eighth Edition. Fcp. 3s. 6d.

Sketch of the History of the Church of England to the Revolution of 1688. By the Right Rev. T. V. SHORT, D.D. Lord Bishop of St. Asaph. Sixth Edition. Crown 8vo. 10s. 6d.

History of the Early Church, from the First Preaching of the Gospel to the Council of Nicæa, A.D. 325. By the Author of 'Amy Herbert.' Fcp. 4s. 6d.

The English Reformation. By F. C. MASSINGBERD, M.A. Chancellor of Lincoln and Rector of South Ormsby. Third Edition, revised and enlarged. Fcp. 6s.

History of Wesleyan Methodism. By GEORGE SMITH, F.A.S. Fourth Edition, with numerous Portraits. 3 vo's. crown 8vo. 7s. each.

Villari's History of Savonarola and of his Times, translated from the Italian by LEONARD HORNER, F.R.S. with the co-operation of the Author. 2 vols. post 8vo. with Medallion, 18s.

Lectures on the History of Modern Music, delivered at the Royal Institution. By JOHN HULLAH, Professor of Vocal Music in King's College and in Queen's College, London. FIRST COURSE, with Chronological Tables, post 8vo. 6s. 6d. SECOND COURSE, on the Transition Period, with 26 Specimens, 8vo. 16s.

Biography and Memoirs.

Letters and Life of Francis Bacon, including all his Occasional Works. Collected and edited, with a Commentary, by J. SPEDDING, Trin. Coll. Cantab. VOLS. I. and II. 8vo. 24s.

Passages from the Life of a Philosopher. By CHARLES BABBAGE, Esq. M.A. F.R.S. &c. 8vo. 12s.

Life of Robert Stephenson, F.R.S. By J. C. JEAFFRESON, Barrister-at-Law, and WILLIAM POLE, F.R.S. Memb. Inst. Civ. Eng. With 2 Portraits and 17 Illustrations. 2 vols. 8vo. 32s.

Life of the Duke of Wellington. By the Rev. G. R. GLEIG, M.A. Popular Edition, carefully revised; with copious Additions. Crown 8vo. with Portrait, 5s.

Brialmont and Gleig's Life of the Duke of Wellington. 4 vols. 8vo. with Illustrations, £2 14s.

Life of the Duke of Wellington, partly from the French of M. BRIALMONT, partly from Original Documents. By the Rev. G. R. GLEIG, M.A. 8vo. with Portrait, 15s.

History of my Religious Opinions. By J. H. NEWMAN, D.D. Being the Substance of Apologia pro Vitâ Suâ. Post 8vo. 6s.

Father Mathew: a Biography. By JOHN FRANCIS MAGUIRE, M.P. Popular Edition, with Portrait. Crown 8vo. 3s. 6d.

Rome; its Rulers and its Institutions. By the same Author. New Edition in preparation.

Memoirs, Miscellanies, and Letters of the late Lucy Aikin; including those addressed to Dr. Channing from 1826 to 1842. Edited by P. H. LE BRETON. Post 8vo. 8s. 6d.

Life of Amelia Wilhelmina Sieveking, from the German. Edited, with the Author's sanction, by CATHERINE WINKWORTH. Post 8vo. with Portrait, 12s.

Louis Spohr's Autobiography. Translated from the German. 8vo. 14s.

Felix Mendelssohn's Letters from *Italy and Switzerland,* and *Letters from 1833 to 1847,* translated by Lady WALLACE. New Edition, with Portrait. 2 vols. crown 8vo. 5s. each.

Diaries of a Lady of Quality, from 1797 to 1844. Edited, with Notes, by A. HAYWARD, Q.C. Post 8vo. 10s. 6d.

Recollections of the late William Wilberforce, M.P. for the County of York during nearly 30 Years. By J. S. HARFORD, F.R.S. Second Edition. Post 8vo. 7s.

Memoirs of Sir Henry Havelock, K.C.B. By JOHN CLARK MARSHMAN. Second Edition. 8vo. with Portrait, 12s. 6d.

Thomas Moore's Memoirs, Journal, and Correspondence. Edited and abridged from the First Edition by Earl RUSSELL. Square crown 8vo. with 8 Portraits, 12s. 6d.

Memoir of the Rev. Sydney Smith. By his Daughter, Lady HOLLAND. With a Selection from his Letters, edited by Mrs. AUSTIN. 2 vols. 8vo. 28s.

Vicissitudes of Families. By Sir BERNARD BURKE, Ulster King of Arms. FIRST, SECOND, and THIRD SERIES. 3 vols. crown 8vo. 12s. 6d. each.

Essays in Ecclesiastical Biography. By the Right Hon. Sir J. STEPHEN, LL.D. Fourth Edition. 8vo. 14s.

Biographical Sketches. By NASSAU W. SENIOR. Post 8vo. 10s. 6d.

Biographies of Distinguished Scientific Men. By FRANÇOIS ARAGO. Translated by Admiral W. H. SMYTH, F.R.S. the Rev. B. POWELL, M.A. and R. GRANT, M.A. 8vo. 18s.

Maunder's Biographical Treasury: Memoirs, Sketches, and Brief Notices of above 12,000 Eminent Persons of All Ages and Nations. Fcp. 8vo. 10s.

Criticism, Philosophy, Polity, &c.

Papinian: a Dialogue on State Affairs between a Constitutional Lawyer and a Country Gentleman about to enter Public Life. By GEORGE ATKINSON, B.A. Oxon. Serjeant-at-Law. Post 8vo. 5s.

On Representative Government. By JOHN STUART MILL. Third Edition 8vo. 9s. crown 8vo. 2s.

On Liberty. By the same Author. Third, Edition. Post 8vo. 7s. 6d. crown 8vo. 1s. 4d.

Principles of Political Economy. By the same. Sixth Edition. 2 vols. 8vo. 30s. or in 1 vol. crown 8vo. 5s.

A System of Logic, Ratiocinative and Inductive. By the same. Fifth Edition. 2 vols. 8vo. 25s.

Utilitarianism. By the same. 2d Edit. 8vo. 5s.

Dissertations and Discussions. By the same Author. 2 vols. 8vo. 24s.

Examination of Sir W. Hamilton's Philosophy, and of the Principal Philosophical Questions discussed in his Writings. By the same Author. 8vo. 14s.

Lord Bacon's Works, collected and edited by R. L. ELLIS, M.A. J. SPEDDING, M.A. and D. D. HEATH. VOLS. I. to V. *Philosophical Works*, 5 vols. 8vo. £4 6s. VOLS. VI. and VII. *Literary and Professional Works*, 2 vols. £1 16s.

Bacon's Essays, with Annotations. By R. WHATELY, D.D. late Archbishop of Dublin. Sixth Edition. 8vo. 10s. 6d.

Elements of Logic. By R. WHATELY, D.D. late Archbishop of Dublin. Ninth Edition. 8vo. 10s. 6d. crown 8vo. 4s. 6d.

Elements of Rhetoric. By the same Author. Seventh Edition. 8vo. 10s. 6d. crown 8vo. 4s. 6d.

English Synonymes. Edited by Archbishop WHATELY. 5th Edition. Fcp. 3s.

Miscellaneous Remains from the Common-place Book of RICHARD WHATELY, D.D. late Archbishop of Dublin. Edited by Miss E. J. WHATELY. Post 8vo. 7s. 6d.

Essays on the Administrations of Great Britain from 1783 to 1830. By the Right Hon. Sir G. C. LEWIS, Bart. Edited by the Right Hon. Sir E. HEAD, Bart. 8vo. with Portrait, 15s.

By the same Author.

A Dialogue on the Best Form of Government, 4s. 6d.

Essay on the Origin and Formation of the Romance Languages, 7s. 6d.

Historical Survey of the Astronomy of the Ancients, 15s.

Inquiry into the Credibility of the Early Roman History, 2 vols. 30s.

On the Methods of Observation and Reasoning in Politics, 2 vols. 28s.

Irish Disturbances and Irish Church Question, 12s.

Remarks on the Use and Abuse of some Political Terms, 9s.

On Foreign Jurisdiction and Extradition of Criminals, 2s. 6d.

The Fables of Babrius, Greek Text with Latin Notes, PART I. 5s. 6d. PART II. 3s. 6d.

Suggestions for the Application of the Egyptological Method to Modern History, 1s.

An Outline of the Necessary Laws of Thought: a Treatise on Pure and Applied Logic. By the Most Rev. W. THOMSON, D.D. Archbishop of York. Crown 8vo. 5s. 6d.

The Elements of Logic. By THOMAS SHEDDEN, M.A. of St. Peter's Coll. Cantab. 12mo. 4s. 6d.

Analysis of Mr. Mill's System of Logic. By W. STEBBING, M.A. Fellow of Worcester College, Oxford. 12mo. 3s. 6d.

The Election of Representatives, Parliamentary and Municipal; a Treatise. By THOMAS HARE, Barrister-at-Law. Third Edition, with Additions. Crown 8vo. 6s.

Speeches of the Right Hon. Lord MACAULAY, corrected by Himself. 8vo. 12s.

Lord Macaulay's Speeches on Parliamentary Reform in 1831 and 1832. 16mo. 1s.

A Dictionary of the English Language. By R. G. LATHAM, M.A. M.D. F.R.S. Founded on the Dictionary of Dr. S. JOHNSON, as edited by the Rev. H. J. TODD, with numerous Emendations and Additions. Publishing in 36 Parts, price 3s. 6d. each, to form 2 vols. 4to.

Thesaurus of English Words and Phrases, classified and arranged so as to facilitate the Expression of Ideas, and assist in Literary Composition. By P. M. ROGET, M.D. 14th Edition, crown 8vo. 10s. 6d.

Lectures on the Science of Language, delivered at the Royal Institution. By MAX MÜLLER, M.A. Taylorian Professor in the University of Oxford. FIRST SERIES, Fourth Edition, 12s. SECOND SERIES, 18s.

The Debater; a Series of Complete Debates, Outlines of Debates, and Questions for Discussion. By F. ROWTON. Fcp. 6s.

A Course of English Reading, adapted to every taste and capacity; or, How and What to Read. By the Rev. J. PYCROFT, B.A. Fourth Edition, fcp. 5s.

Manual of English Literature, Historical and Critical: with a Chapter on English Metres. By THOMAS ARNOLD, B.A. Post 8vo. 10s. 6d.

Southey's Doctor, complete in One Volume. Edited by the Rev. J.W. WARTER, B.D. Square crown 8vo. 12s. 6d.

Historical and Critical Commentary on the Old Testament; with a New Translation. By M. M. KALISCH, Ph. D. VOL. I. *Genesis*, 8vo. 18s. or adapted for the General Reader, 12s. VOL. II. *Exodus*, 15s. or adapted for the General Reader, 12s.

A Hebrew Grammar, with Exercises. By the same. PART I. *Outlines with Exercises*, 8vo. 12s. 6d. KEY, 5s. PART II. *Exceptional Forms and Constructions*, 12s. 6d.

A Latin-English Dictionary. By J. T. WHITE, M.A. of Corpus Christi College, and J. E. RIDDLE, M.A. of St. Edmund Hall, Oxford. Imp. 8vo. pp. 2,128, 42s.

A New Latin-English Dictionary, abridged from the larger work of *White* and *Riddle* (as above), by J. T. WHITE, M.A. Joint-Author. Medium 8vo. pp. 1,048, 18s.

A Diamond Latin-English Dictionary, or Guide to the Meaning, Quality, and Accentuation of Latin Classical Words. By J. E. RIDDLE, M.A. 32mo. 2s. 6d.

An English-Greek Lexicon, containing all the Greek Words used by Writers of good authority. By C. D. YONGE, B.A. Fifth Edition. 4to. 21s.

Mr. Yonge's New Lexicon, English and Greek, abridged from his larger work (as above). Square 12mo. 8s. 6d.

A Greek-English Lexicon. Compiled by H. G. LIDDELL, D.D. Dean of Christ Church, and R. SCOTT, D.D. Master of Balliol. Fifth Edition, crown 4to. 31s. 6d.

A Lexicon, Greek and English, abridged from LIDDELL and SCOTT's *Greek-English Lexicon*. Eleventh Edition, square 12mo. 7s. 6d.

A Practical Dictionary of the French and English Languages. By L. CONTANSEAU. 8th Edition, post 8vo. 10s. 6d.

Contanseau's Pocket Dictionary, French and English, abridged from the above by the Author. New Edition. 18mo. 5s.

New Practical Dictionary of the German Language; German-English, and English-German. By the Rev. W. L. BLACKLEY, M.A., and Dr. CARL MARTIN FRIEDLANDER. Post 8vo. [*In the press.*

Miscellaneous Works and Popular Metaphysics.

Recreations of a Country Parson: being a Selection of the Contributions of A. K. H. B. to *Fraser's Magazine*. SECOND SERIES. Crown 8vo. 3s. 6d.

The Commonplace Philosopher in Town and Country. By the same Author. Crown 8vo. 3s. 6d.

Leisure Hours in Town; Essays Consolatory, Æsthetical, Moral, Social, and Domestic. By the same. Crown 8vo. 3s. 6d.

The Autumn Holidays of a Country Parson: Essays contributed to *Fraser's Magazine* and to *Good Words*, by the same. Crown 8vo. 3s. 6d.

The Graver Thoughts of a Country Parson, SECOND SERIES. By the same. Crown 8vo. 3s. 6d.

Critical Essays of a Country Parson, selected from Essays contributed to *Fraser's Magazine,* by the same. Post 8vo. 9s.

A Campaigner at Home. By SHIRLEY, Author of 'Thalatta,' and 'Nugæ Criticæ.' Post 8vo. with Vignette, 7s. 6d.

Friends in Council: a Series of Readings and Discourses thereon. 2 vols. fcp. 9s.

Friends in Council, SECOND SERIES. 2 vols. post 8vo. 14s.

Essays written in the Intervals of Business. Fcp. 2s. 6d.

Lord Macaulay's Miscellaneous Writings.

LIBRARY EDITION, 2 vols. 8vo. Portrait, 21s.

PEOPLE'S EDITION, 1 vol. crown 8vo. 4s. 6d.

The Rev. Sydney Smith's Miscellaneous Works; including his Contributions to the *Edinburgh Review*.

LIBRARY EDITION, 3 vols. 8vo. 36s.

TRAVELLER'S EDITION, in 1 vol. 21s.

In POCKET VOLUMES, 3 vols. fcp. 21s.

PEOPLE'S EDITION, 2 vols. crown 8vo. 8s.

Elementary Sketches of Moral Philosophy, delivered at the Royal Institution. By the same Author. Fcp. 7s.

The Wit and Wisdom of the Rev. SYDNEY SMITH: a Selection of the most memorable Passages in his Writings and Conversation. 16mo. 7s. 6d.

The History of the Supernatural in All Ages and Nations, and in All Churches, Christian and Pagan; demonstrating a Universal Faith. By WILLIAM HOWITT. 2 vols. post 8vo. 18s.

The Superstitions of Witchcraft. By HOWARD WILLIAMS, M.A. St. John's Coll. Camb. Post 8vo. 7s. 6d.

Chapters on Mental Physiology. By Sir HENRY HOLLAND, Bart. M.D. F.R.S. Second Edition. Post 8vo. 8s. 6d.

Essays selected from Contributions to the *Edinburgh Review*. By HENRY ROGERS. Second Edition. 3 vols. fcp. 21s.

The Eclipse of Faith; or, a Visit to a Religious Sceptic. By the same Author. Tenth Edition. Fcp. 5s.

Defence of the Eclipse of Faith, by its Author; a Rejoinder to Dr. Newman's *Reply*. Third Edition. Fcp. 3s. 6d.

Selections from the Correspondence of R. E. H. Greyson. By the same Author. Third Edition. Crown 8vo. 7s. 6d.

Fulleriana, or the Wisdom and Wit of THOMAS FULLER, with Essay on his Life and Genius. By the same Author. 16mo. 2s. 6d.

The Secret of Hegel: being the Hegelian System in Origin, Principle, Form, and Matter. By JAMES HUTCHISON STIRLING. 2 vols. 8vo. 28s.

An Introduction to Mental Philosophy, on the Inductive Method. By J. D. MORELL, M.A. LL.D. 8vo. 12s.

Elements of Psychology, containing the Analysis of the Intellectual Powers. By the same Author. Post 8vo. 7s. 6d.

Sight and Touch: an Attempt to Disprove the Received (or Berkeleian) Theory of Vision. By THOMAS K. ABBOTT, M.A. Fellow and Tutor of Trin. Coll. Dublin. 8vo. with 21 Woodcuts, 5s. 6d.

The Senses and the Intellect. By ALEXANDER BAIN, M.A. Prof. of Logic in the Univ. of Aberdeen. Second Edition. 8vo. 15s.

The Emotions and the Will, by the same Author; completing a Systematic Exposition of the Human Mind. 8vo. 15s.

On the Study of Character, including an Estimate of Phrenology. By the same Author. 8vo. 9s.

Time and Space: a Metaphysical Essay. By SHADWORTH H. HODGSON. 8vo. pp. 588, price 16s.

Hours with the Mystics: a Contribution to the History of Religious Opinion. By ROBERT ALFRED VAUGHAN, B.A. Second Edition. 2 vols. crown 8vo. 12s.

Psychological Inquiries. By the late Sir BENJ. C. BRODIE, Bart. 2 vols. or SERIES, fcp. 5s. each.

The Philosophy of Necessity; or, Natural Law as applicable to Mental, Moral, and Social Science. By CHARLES BRAY. Second Edition. 8vo. 9s.

The Education of the Feelings and Affections. By the same Author. Third Edition. 8vo. 3s. 6d.

Christianity and Common Sense. By Sir WILLOUGHBY JONES, Bart. M.A. Trin. Coll. Cantab. 8vo. 6s.

Astronomy, Meteorology, Popular Geography, &c.

Outlines of Astronomy. By Sir J. F. W. HERSCHEL, Bart, M.A. Seventh Edition, revised; with Plates and Woodcuts. 8vo. 18s.

Arago's Popular Astronomy. Translated by Admiral W. H. SMYTH, F.R.S. and R. GRANT, M.A. With 25 Plates and 358 Woodcuts. 2 vols. 8vo. £2 5s.

Arago's Meteorological Essays, with Introduction by Baron HUMBOLDT. Translated under the superintendence of Major-General E. SABINE, R.A. 8vo. 18s.

Saturn and its System. By RICHARD A. PROCTOR, B.A. late Scholar of St. John's Coll. Camb. and King's Coll. London. 8vo. with 14 Plates, 14s.

The Weather-Book; a Manual of Practical Meteorology. By Rear-Admiral ROBERT FITZ ROY, R.N. F.R.S. Third Edition, with 16 Diagrams. 8vo. 15s.

Saxby's Weather System, or Lunar Influence on Weather. By S. M. SAXBY, R.N. Instructor of Naval Engineers. Second Edition. Post 8vo. 4s.

Dove's Law of Storms considered in connexion with the ordinary Movements of the Atmosphere. Translated by R. H. SCOTT, M.A. T.C.D. 8vo. 10s. 6d.

Celestial Objects for Common Telescopes. By T. W. WEBB, M.A. F.R.A.S. With Map of the Moon, and Woodcuts. 16mo. 7s.

Physical Geography for Schools and General Readers. By M. F. MAURY, LL.D. Fcp. with 2 Charts, 2s. 6d.

A Dictionary, Geographical, Statistical, and Historical, of the various Countries, Places, and principal Natural Objects in the World. By J. R. M'CULLOCH. With 6 Maps. 2 vols. 8vo. 63s.

A General Dictionary of Geography, Descriptive, Physical, Statistical, and Historical; forming a complete Gazetteer of the World. By A. KEITH JOHNSTON, F.R.S.E. 8vo. 31s. 6d.

A Manual of Geography, Physical, Industrial, and Political. By W. HUGHES, F.R.G.S. Prof. of Geog. in King's Coll. and in Queen's Coll. Lond. With 6 Maps. Fcp. 7s. 6d.

The Geography of British History; a Geographical Description of the British Islands at Successive Periods. By the same. With 6 Maps. Fcp. 8s. 6d.

Abridged Text-Book of British Geography. By the same. Fcp. 1s. 6d.

The British Empire; a Sketch of the Geography, Growth, Natural and Political Features of the United Kingdom, its Colonies and Dependencies. By CAROLINE BRAY. With 5 Maps. Fcp. 7s. 6d.

Colonisation and Colonies: a Series of Lectures delivered before the University of Oxford. By HERMAN MERIVALE, M.A. Prof. of Polit. Econ. 8vo. 18s.

Maunder's Treasury of Geography, Physical, Historical, Descriptive, and Political. Edited by W. HUGHES, F.R.G.S. With 7 Maps and 16 Plates. Fcp. 10s.

Natural History and Popular Science.

The Elements of Physics or Natural Philosophy. By NEIL ARNOTT, M.D. F.R.S. Physician Extraordinary to the Queen. Sixth Edition. PART I. 8vo. 10s. 6d.

Heat Considered as a Mode of Motion. By Professor JOHN TYNDALL, F.R.S. LL.D. Second Edition. Crown 8vo. with Woodcuts, 12s. 6d.

Volcanos, the Character of their Phenomena, their Share in the Structure and Composition of the Surface of the Globe, &c. By G. POULETT SCROPE, M.P. F.R.S. Second Edition. 8vo. with Illustrations, 15s.

A Treatise on Electricity, in Theory and Practice. By A. DE LA RIVE, Prof. in the Academy of Geneva. Translated by C. V. WALKER, F.R.S. 3 vols. 8vo. with Woodcuts, £3 13s.

The Correlation of Physical Forces. By W. R. GROVE, Q.C. V.P.R.S. Fourth Edition. 8vo. 7s. 6d.

The Geological Magazine; or, Monthly Journal of Geology. Edited by HENRY WOODWARD, F.G.S. F.Z.S. British Museum; assisted by Professor J. MORRIS, F.G.S. and R. ETHERIDGE, F.R.S.E. F.G.S. 8vo. price 1s. monthly.

A Guide to Geology. By J. PHILLIPS, M.A. Prof. of Geol. in the Univ. of Oxford. Fifth Edition; with Plates and Diagrams. Fcp. 4s.

A Glossary of Mineralogy. By H. W. BRISTOW, F.G.S. of the Geological Survey of Great Britain. With 486 Figures. Crown 8vo. 12s.

Phillips's Elementary Introduction to Mineralogy, with extensive Alterations and Additions, by H. J. BROOKE, F.R.S. and W. H. MILLER, F.G.S. Post 8vo. with Woodcuts, 18s.

Van Der Hoeven's Handbook of ZOOLOGY. Translated from the Second Dutch Edition by the Rev. W. CLARK, M.D. F.R.S. 2 vols. 8vo. with 24 Plates of Figures, 60s.

The Comparative Anatomy and Physiology of the Vertebrate Animals. By RICHARD OWEN, F.R.S. D.C.L. 2 vols. 8vo. with upwards of 1,200 Woodcuts.
[*In the press.*

Homes without Hands: an Account of the Habitations constructed by various Animals, classed according to their Principles of Construction. By Rev. J. G. WOOD, M.A. F.L.S. Illustrations on Wood by G. Pearson, from Drawings by F. W. Keyl and E. A. Smith. In 20 Parts, 1s. each.

Manual of Corals and Sea Jellies. By J. R. GREENE, B.A. Edited by the Rev. J. A. GALBRAITH, M.A. and the Rev. S. HAUGHTON, M.D. Fcp. with 39 Woodcuts, 5s.

Manual of Sponges and Animalculæ; with a General Introduction on the Principles of Zoology. By the same Author and Editors. Fcp. with 16 Woodcuts, 2s.

Manual of the Metalloids. By J. APJOHN, M.D. F.R.S. and the same Editors. Fcp. with 38 Woodcuts, 7s. 6d.

The Sea and its Living Wonders. By Dr. G. HARTWIG. Second (English) Edition. 8vo. with many Illustrations, 18s.

The Tropical World. By the same Author. With 8 Chromoxylographs and 172 Woodcuts. 8vo. 21s.

Sketches of the Natural History of Ceylon. By Sir J. EMERSON TENNENT, K.C.S. LL.D. With 82 Wood Engravings. Post 8vo. 12s. 6d.

Ceylon. By the same Author. 5th Edition; with Maps, &c. and 90 Wood Engravings. 2 vols. 8vo. £2 10s.

A Familiar History of Birds. By E. STANLEY, D.D. F.R.S. late Lord Bishop of Norwich. Seventh Edition, with Woodcuts. Fcp. 3s. 6d.

Marvels and Mysteries of Instinct; or, Curiosities of Animal Life. By G. GARRATT. Third Edition. Fcp. 7s.

Home Walks and Holiday Rambles. By the Rev. C. A. JOHNS, B.A. F.L.S. Fcp. with 10 Illustrations, 6s.

Kirby and Spence's Introduction to Entomology, or Elements of the Natural History of Insects. Seventh Edition. Crown 8vo. 5s.

Maunder's Treasury of Natural History, or Popular Dictionary of Zoology. Revised and corrected by T. S. COBBOLD, M.D. Fcp. with 900 Woodcuts, 10s.

The Treasury of Botany, on the Plan of Maunder's Treasury. By J. LINDLEY, M.D. and T. MOORE, F.L.S. assisted by other Practical Botanists. With 16 Plates, and many Woodcuts from designs by W. H. Fitch. Fcp. [*In the press.*

The Rose Amateur's Guide. By THOMAS RIVERS. 8th Edition. Fcp. 4s.

The British Flora; comprising the Phænogamous or Flowering Plants and the Ferns. By Sir W. J. HOOKER, K.H. and G. A. WALKER-ARNOTT, LL.D. 12mo. with 12 Plates, 14s. or coloured, 21s.

Bryologia Britannica; containing the Mosses of Great Britain and Ireland, arranged and described. By W. WILSON. 8vo. with 61 Plates, 42s. or coloured, £4 4s.

The Indoor Gardener. By Miss MALING. Fcp. with Frontispiece, 5s.

Loudon's Encyclopædia of Plants; comprising the Specific Character, Description, Culture, History, &c. of all the Plants found in Great Britain. With upwards of 12,000 Woodcuts. 8vo. £3 13s. 6d.

Loudon's Encyclopædia of Trees and Shrubs; containing the Hardy Trees and Shrubs of Great Britain scientifically and popularly described. With 2,000 Woodcuts. 8vo. 50s.

Maunder's Scientific and Literary Treasury; a Popular Encyclopædia of Science, Literature, and Art. Fcp. 10s.

A Dictionary of Science, Literature, and Art. Fourth Edition. Edited by W. T. BRANDE, D.C.L. and GEORGE W. COX, M.A., assisted by gentlemen of eminent Scientific and Literary Acquirements. In 12 Parts, each containing 240 pages, price 5s. forming 3 vols. medium 8vo. price 21s. each.

Essays on Scientific and other subjects, contributed to Reviews. By Sir H. HOLLAND, Bart. M.D. Second Edition. 8vo. 14s.

Essays from the Edinburgh and *Quarterly Reviews*; with Addresses and other Pieces. By Sir J. F. W. HERSCHEL, Bart. M.A. 8vo. 18s.

Chemistry, Medicine, Surgery, and the Allied Sciences.

A Dictionary of Chemistry and the Allied Branches of other Sciences. By HENRY WATTS, F.C.S. assisted by eminent Contributors. 5 vols. medium 8vo. in course of publication in Parts. VOL. I. 3s. 6d. VOL. II. 26s. and VOL. III. 31s. 6d. are now ready.

Handbook of Chemical Analysis, adapted to the Unitary System of Notation: By F. T. CONINGTON, M.A. F.C.S. Post 8vo. 7s. 6d. — TABLES of QUALITATIVE ANALYSIS adapted to the same, 2s. 6d.

A Handbook of Volumetrical Analysis. By ROBERT H. SCOTT, M.A. T.C.D. Post 8vo. 4s. 6d.

Elements of Chemistry, Theoretical and Practical. By WILLIAM A. MILLER, M.D. LL.D. F.R.S. F.G.S. Professor of Chemistry, King's College, London. 3 vols. 8vo. £2 13s. PART I. CHEMICAL PHYSICS, Third Edition, 12s. PART II. INORGANIC CHEMISTRY, 21s. PART III. ORGANIC CHEMISTRY, Second Edition, 20s.

A Manual of Chemistry, Descriptive and Theoretical. By WILLIAM ODLING, M.B. F.R.S. Lecturer on Chemistry at St. Bartholomew's Hospital. PART I. 8vo. 9s.

A Course of Practical Chemistry, for the use of Medical Students. By the same Author. Second Edition, with 70 new Woodcuts. Crown 8vo. 7s. 6d.

The Diagnosis and Treatment of the Diseases of Women; including the Diagnosis of Pregnancy. By GRAILY HEWITT, M.D. Physician to the British Lying-in Hospital. 8vo. 16s.

Lectures on the Diseases of Infancy and Childhood. By CHARLES WEST, M.D. &c. 5th Edition, revised and enlarged. 8vo. 16s.

Exposition of the Signs and Symptoms of Pregnancy: with other Papers on subjects connected with Midwifery. By W. F. MONTGOMERY, M.A. M.D. M.R.I.A. 8vo. with Illustrations, 25s.

A System of Surgery, Theoretical and Practical, in Treatises by Various Authors. Edited by T. HOLMES, M.A. Cantab. Assistant-Surgeon to St. George's Hospital. 4 vols. 8vo. £4 13s.

Vol. I. General Pathology, 21s.

Vol. II. Local Injuries: Gun-shot Wounds, Injuries of the Head, Back, Face, Neck, Chest, Abdomen, Pelvis, of the Upper and Lower Extremities, and Diseases of the Eye. 21s.

Vol. III. Operative Surgery. Diseases of the Organs of Circulation, Locomotion, &c. 21s.

Vol. IV. Diseases of the Organs of Digestion, of the Genito-Urinary System, and of the Breast, Thyroid Gland, and Skin; with APPENDIX and GENERAL INDEX. 30s.

Lectures on the Principles and Practice of Physic. By THOMAS WATSON, M.D. Physician-Extraordinary to the Queen. Fourth Edition. 2 vols. 8vo. 34s.

Lectures on Surgical Pathology. By J. PAGET, F.R.S. Surgeon-Extraordinary to the Queen. Edited by W. TURNER, M.B. 8vo. with 117 Woodcuts, 21s.

A Treatise on the Continued Fevers of Great Britain. By C. MURCHISON, M.D. Senior Physician to the London Fever Hospital. 8vo. with coloured Plates, 18s.

Anatomy, Descriptive and Surgical. By HENRY GRAY, F.R.S. With 410 Wood Engravings from Dissections. Third Edition, by T. HOLMES, M.A. Cantab. Royal 8vo. 28s.

The Cyclopædia of Anatomy and Physiology. Edited by the late R. B. TODD, M.D. F.R.S. Assisted by nearly all the most eminent cultivators of Physiological Science of the present age. 5 vols. 8vo. with 2,853 Woodcuts, £6 6s.

Physiological Anatomy and Physiology of Man. By the late R. B. TODD, M.D. F.R.S. and W. BOWMAN, F.R.S. of King's College. With numerous Illustrations. VOL. II. 8vo. 25s.

A Dictionary of Practical Medicine. By J. COPLAND, M.D. F.R.S. Abridged from the larger work by the Author, assisted by J. C. COPLAND, M.R.C.S. 1 vol. 8vo. [*In the press.*

Dr. Copland's Dictionary of Practical Medicine (the larger work). 3 vols. 8vo. £5 11s.

The Works of Sir B. C. Brodie, Bart. collected and arranged by CHARLES HAWKINS, F.R.C.S.E. 3 vols. 8vo. with Medallion and Facsimile, 48s.

Autobiography of Sir B. C. Brodie, Bart. printed from the Author's materials left in MS. Fcp. 4s. 6d.

Medical Notes and Reflections. By Sir H. HOLLAND, Bart. M.D. Third Edition. 8vo. 18s.

A Manual of Materia Medica and Therapeutics, abridged from Dr. PEREIRA's *Elements* by F. J. FARRE, M.D. Cantab. assisted by R. BENTLEY, M.R.C.S. and by R. WARINGTON, F.C.S. 1 vol. 8vo. [*In October.*

Dr. Pereira's Elements of Materia Medica and Therapeutics, Third Edition, by A. S. TAYLOR, M.D. and G. O. REES, M.D 3 vols. 8vo. with Woodcuts, £3 15s.

Thomson's Conspectus of the British Pharmacopœia. Twenty-fourth Edition, corrected and made conformable throughout to the New Pharmacopœia of the General Council of Medical Education. By E. LLOYD BIRKETT, M.D. 18mo. 5s. 6d.

Manual of the Domestic Practice of Medicine. By W. B. KESTEVEN, F.R.C.S.E. Second Edition, thoroughly revised, with Additions. Fcp. 5s.

The Fine Arts, and Illustrated Editions.

The New Testament, illustrated with Wood Engravings after the Early Masters, chiefly of the Italian School. Crown 4to. 63s. cloth, gilt top; or £5 5s. elegantly bound in morocco.

Lyra Germanica; Hymns for the Sundays and Chief Festivals of the Christian Year. Translated by CATHERINE WINKWORTH; 125 Illustrations on Wood drawn by J. LEIGHTON, F.S.A. Fcp. 4to. 21s.

NEW WORKS PUBLISHED BY LONGMANS AND CO. 11

Cats' and Farlie's Moral Emblems; with Aphorisms, Adages, and Proverbs of all Nations : comprising 121 Illustrations on Wood by J. LEIGHTON, F.S.A. with an appropriate Text by R. PIGOT. Imperial 8vo. 31s. 6d.

Bunyan's Pilgrim's Progress: with 126 Illustrations on Steel and Wood by C. BENNETT; and a Preface by the Rev. C. KINGSLEY. Fcp. 4to. 21s.

Shakspeare's Sentiments and Similes printed in Black and Gold and illuminated in the Missal style by HENRY NOEL HUMPHREYS. In massive covers, containing the Medallion and Cypher of Shakspeare. Square post 8vo. 21s.

The History of Our Lord, as exemplified in Works of Art; with that of His Types in the Old and New Testament. By Mrs. JAMESON and Lady EASTLAKE. Being the concluding Series of 'Sacred and Legendary Art;' with 13 Etchings and 281 Woodcuts. 2 vols. square crown 8vo. 42s.

In the same Series, by Mrs. JAMESON.

Legends of the Saints and Martyrs. Fourth Edition, with 19 Etchings and 187 Woodcuts. 2 vols. 31s. 6d.

Legends of the Monastic Orders. Third Edition, with 11 Etchings and 88 Woodcuts. 1 vol. 21s.

Legends of the Madonna. Third Edition. with 27 Etchings and 165 Woodcuts. 1 vol. 21s.

Arts, Manufactures, &c.

Encyclopædia of Architecture, Historical, Theoretical, and Practical. By JOSEPH GWILT. With more than 1,000 Woodcuts. 8vo. 42s.

Tuscan Sculptors, their Lives, Works, and Times. With 45 Etchings and 28 Woodcuts from Original Drawings and Photographs. By CHARLES C. PERKINS 2 vols. imp. 8vo. 63s.

The Engineer's Handbook; explaining the Principles which should guide the young Engineer in the Construction of Machinery. By C. S. LOWNDES. Post 8vo. 5s.

The Elements of Mechanism. By T. M. GOODEVE, M.A. Prof. of Mechanics at the R M. Acad. Woolwich. Second Edition, with 217 Woodcuts. Post 8vo. 6s. 6d.

Ure's Dictionary of Arts, Manufactures, and Mines. Re-written and enlarged by ROBERT HUNT, F.R.S., assisted by numerous gentlemen eminent in Science and the Arts. With 2,000 Woodcuts. 3 vols. 8vo. £4.

Encyclopædia of Civil Engineering, Historical, Theoretical, and Practical. By E. CRESY, .C.E. With above 3,000 Woodcuts. 8vo. 42s.

Treatise on Mills and Millwork. By W. FAIRBAIRN, C.E. F.R.S. With 18 Plates and 322 Woodcuts. 2 vols. 8vo. 32s.

Useful Information for Engineers. By the same Author. FIRST and SECOND SERIES, with many Plates and Woodcuts. 2 vols. crown 8vo. 10s. 6d. each.

The Application of Cast and Wrought Iron to Building Purposes. By the same Author. Third Edition, with 6 Plates and 118 Woodcuts. 8vo. 16s.

The Practical Mechanic's Journal: An Illustrated Record of Mechanical and Engineering Science, and Epitome of Patent Inventions. 4to. price 1s. monthly.

The Practical Draughtsman's Book of Industrial Design. By W. JOHNSON, Assoc. Inst. C.E. With many hundred Illustrations. 4to. 28s. 6d.

The Patentee's Manual: a Treatise on the Law and Practice of Letters Patent for the use of Patentees and Inventors. By J. and J. H. JOHNSON. Post 8vo. 7s. 6d.

The Artisan Club's Treatise on the Steam Engine, in its various Applications to Mines, Mills, Steam Navigation, Railways, and Agriculture. By J. BOURNE, C.E. Sixth Edition; with 37 Plates and 546 Woodcuts. 4to. 42s.

Catechism of the Steam Engine, in its various Applications to Mines, Mills, Steam Navigation, Railways, and Agriculture. By J. BOURNE, C.E. With 199 Woodcuts. Fcp. 9s. The INTRODUCTION of 'Recent Improvements' may be had separately, with 110 Woodcuts, price 3s. 6d.

Handbook of the Steam Engine, by the same Author, forming a KEY to the Catechism of the Steam Engine, with 67 Woodcuts. Fcp. 9s.

The Theory of War Illustrated by numerous Examples from History. By Lieut.-Col. P. L. MACDOUGALL. Third Edition, with 10 Plans. Post 8vo. 10s. 6d.

Collieries and Colliers ; A Handbook of the Law and leading Cases relating thereto. By J. C. FOWLER, Barrister-at-Law, Stipendiary Magistrate. Fcp. 6s.

The Art of Perfumery ; the History and Theory of Odours, and the Methods of Extracting the Aromas of Plants. By Dr. PIESSE, F.C.S. Third Edition, with 53 Woodcuts. Crown 8vo. 10s. 6d.

Chemical, Natural, and Physical Magic, for Juveniles during the Holidays. By the same Author. Third Edition, enlarged, with 38 Woodcuts. Fcp. 6s.

The Laboratory of Chemical Wonders: A Scientific Mélange for Young People. By the same. Crown 8vo. 5s. 6d.

Talpa ; or, the Chronicles of a Clay Farm. By C. W. HOSKYNS, Esq. With 24 Woodcuts from Designs by G. CRUIKSHANK. 16mo. 5s. 6d.

H.R.H. the Prince Consort's Farms; an Agricultural Memoir. By JOHN CHALMERS MORTON. Dedicated by permission to Her Majesty the QUEEN. With 40 Wood Engravings. 4to. 52s. 6d.

Loudon's Encyclopædia of Agriculture: Comprising the Laying-out, Improvement, and Management of Landed Property, and the Cultivation and Economy of the Productions of Agriculture. With 1,100 Woodcuts. 8vo. 31s. 6d.

Loudon's Encyclopædia of Gardening: Comprising the Theory and Practice of Horticulture, Floriculture, Arboriculture, and Landscape Gardening. With 1,000 Woodcuts. 8vo. 31s. 6d.

Loudon's Encyclopædia of Cottage, Farm, and Villa Architecture and Furniture. With more than 2,000 Woodcuts. 8vo. 42s.

History of Windsor Great Park and Windsor Forest. By WILLIAM MENZIES, Resident Deputy Surveyor. With 2 Maps and 20 Photographs. Imp. folio, £8 8s.

The Sanitary Management and Utilisation of Sewage: comprising Details of a System applicable to Cottages, Dwelling-Houses, Public Buildings, and Towns; Suggestions relating to the Arterial Drainage of the Country, and the Water Supply of Rivers. By the same Author. Imp. 8vo. with 9 Illustrations, 12s. 6d.

Bayldon's Art of Valuing Rents and Tillages, and Claims of Tenants upon Quitting Farms, both at Michaelmas and Lady-Day. Eighth Edition, revised by J. C. MORTON. 8vo. 10s. 6d.

Religious and Moral Works.

An Exposition of the 39 Articles, Historical and Doctrinal. By E. HAROLD BROWNE, D.D. Lord Bishop of Ely. Sixth Edition, 8vo. 16s.

The Pentateuch and the Elohistic Psalms, in Reply to Bishop Colenso. By the same. Second Edition. 8vo. 2s.

Examination Questions on Bishop Browne's Exposition of the Articles. By the Rev. J. GORLE, M.A. Fcp. 3s. 6d.

Five Lectures on the Character of St. Paul; being the Hulsean Lectures for 1862. By the Rev. J. S. HOWSON, D.D. Second Edition. 8vo. 9s.

The Life and Epistles of St. Paul. By W. J. CONYBEARE, M.A. late Fellow of Trin. Coll. Cantab. and J. S. HOWSON, D.D. Principal of Liverpool Coll.

LIBRARY EDITION, with all the Original Illustrations, Maps, Landscapes on Steel, Woodcuts, &c. 2 vols. 4to. 48s.

INTERMEDIATE EDITION, with a Selection of Maps, Plates, and Woodcuts. 2 vols. square crown 8vo. 31s. 6d.

PEOPLE'S EDITION, revised and condensed, with 46 Illustrations and Maps. 2 vols. crown 8vo. 12s.

The Voyage and Shipwreck of St. Paul; with Dissertations on the Ships and Navigation of the Ancients. By JAMES SMITH, F.R.S. Crown 8vo. Charts, 8s. 6d.

A Critical and Grammatical Commentary on St. Paul's Epistles. By C. J. ELLICOTT, D.D. Lord Bishop of Gloucester and Bristol. 8vo.

Galatians, Third Edition, 8s. 6d.

Ephesians, Third Edition, 8s. 6d.

Pastoral Epistles, Third Edition, 10s. 6d.

Philippians, Colossians, and Philemon, Third Edition, 10s. 6d.

Thessalonians, Second Edition, 7s. 6d.

Historical Lectures on the Life of Our Lord Jesus Christ: being the Hulsean Lectures for 1859. By the same Author. Fourth Edition. 8vo. 10s. 6d.

The Destiny of the Creature; and other Sermons preached before the University of Cambridge. By the same. Post 8vo. 5s.

The Broad and the Narrow Way; Two Sermons preached before the University of Cambridge. By the same. Crown 8vo. 2s.

Rev. T. H. Horne's Introduction to the Critical Study and Knowledge of the Holy Scriptures. Eleventh Edition, corrected, and extended under careful Editorial revision. With 4 Maps and 22 Woodcuts and Facsimiles. 4 vols. 8vo. £3 13s. 6d.

Rev. T. H. Horne's Compendious Introduction to the Study of the Bible, being an Analysis of the larger work by the same Author. Re-edited by the Rev. JOHN AYRE, M.A. With Maps, &c. Post 8vo. 9s.

The Treasury of Bible Knowledge, on the plan of Maunder's Treasuries. By the Rev. JOHN AYRE, M.A. Fcp. 8vo. with Maps and Illustrations. [*In the press.*

The Greek Testament; with Notes, Grammatical and Exegetical. By the Rev. W. WEBSTER, M.A. and the Rev. W. F. WILKINSON, M.A. 2 vols. 8vo. £2 4s.

VOL. I. the Gospels and Acts, 20s.

VOL. II. the Epistles and Apocalypse, 24s.

The Four Experiments in Church and State; and the Conflicts of Churches. By Lord ROBERT MONTAGU, M.P. 8vo. 12s.

Every-day Scripture Difficulties explained and illustrated; Gospels of St. Matthew and St. Mark. By J. E. PRESCOTT, M.A. 8vo. 9s.

The Pentateuch and Book of Joshua Critically Examined. By the Right Rev. J. W. COLENSO, D.D. Lord Bishop of Natal. People's Edition, in 1 vol. crown 8vo. 6s. or in 5 Parts, 1s. each.

The Pentateuch and Book of Joshua Critically Examined. By Prof. A. KUENEN, of Leyden. Translated from the Dutch, and edited with Notes, by the Right Rev. J. W. COLENSO, D.D. Bishop of Natal. 8vo. 8s. 6d.

The Formation of Christendom. PART I. By T. W. ALLIES. 8vo. 12s.

Christendom's Divisions; a Philosophical Sketch of the Divisions of the Christian Family in East and West. By EDMUND S. FFOULKES, formerly Fellow and Tutor of Jesus Coll. Oxford. Post 8vo. 7s. 6d.

The Life of Christ, an Eclectic Gospel, from the Old and New Testaments, arranged on a New Principle, with Analytical Tables, &c. By CHARLES DE LA PRYME, M.A. Trin. Coll. Camb. Revised Edition. 8vo. 5s.

The Hidden Wisdom of Christ and the Key of Knowledge; or, History of the Apocrypha. By ERNEST DE BUNSEN. 2 vols. 8vo. 28s.

Hippolytus and his Age; or, the Beginnings and Prospects of Christianity. By Baron BUNSEN, D.D. 2 vols. 8vo. 30s.

Outlines of the Philosophy of Universal History, applied to Language and Religion: Containing an Account of the Alphabetical Conferences. By the same Author. 2 vols. 8vo. 33s.

Analecta Ante-Nicæna. By the same Author. 3 vols. 8vo. 42s.

Essays on Religion and Literature. By various Writers. Edited by H. E. MANNING, D.D. 8vo. 10s. 6d.

Essays and Reviews. By the Rev. W. TEMPLE, D.D. the Rev. R. WILLIAMS, B.D. the Rev. B. POWELL, M.A. the Rev. H. B. WILSON, B.D. C. W. GOODWIN, M.A. the Rev. M. PATTISON, B.D. and the Rev. B. JOWETT, M.A. 12th Edition. Fcp. 8vo. 5s.

Mosheim's Ecclesiastical History. MURDOCK and SOAMES's Translation and Notes, re-edited by the Rev. W. STUBBS, M.A. 3 vols. 8vo. 45s.

Bishop Jeremy Taylor's Entire Works; With Life by BISHOP HEBER. Revised and corrected by the Rev. C. P. EDEN, 10 vols. £5 5s.

Passing Thoughts on Religion. By the Author of 'Amy Herbert.' 8th Edition. Fcp. 5s.

Thoughts for the Holy Week, for Young Persons. By the same Author. 3d Edition. Fcp. 8vo. 2s.

Night Lessons from Scripture. By the same Author. 2d Edition. 32mo. 3s.

Self-examination before Confirmation. By the same Author. 32mo. 1s. 6d.

Readings for a Month Preparatory to Confirmation from Writers of the Early and English Church. By the same. Fcp. 4s.

Readings for Every Day in Lent, compiled from the Writings of Bishop JEREMY TAYLOR. By the same. Fcp. 5s.

Preparation for the Holy Communion; the Devotions chiefly from the works of JEREMY TAYLOR. By the same. 32mo. 3s.

Morning Clouds. Second Edition. Fcp. 5s.

Spring and Autumn. By the same Author. Post 8vo. 6s.

The Wife's Manual; or, Prayers, Thoughts, and Songs on Several Occasions of a Matron's Life. By the Rev. W. CALVERT, M.A. Crown 8vo. 10s. 6d.

Spiritual Songs for the Sundays and Holidays throughout the Year. By J. S. B. MONSELL, LL.D. Vicar of Egham. Fourth Edition. Fcp. 4s. 6d.

The Beatitudes: Abasement before God: Sorrow for Sin; Meekness of Spirit; Desire for Holiness; Gentleness; Purity of Heart; the Peace-makers; Sufferings for Christ. By the same. 2d Edition, fcp. 3s. 6d.

Hymnologia Christiana; or, Psalms and Hymns selected and arranged in the order of the Christian Seasons. By B. H. KENNEDY, D.D. Prebendary of Lichfield. Crown 8vo. 7s. 6d.

Lyra Domestica; Christian Songs for Domestic Edification. Translated from the *Psaltery and Harp* of C. J. P. SPITTA, and from other sources, by RICHARD MASSIE. FIRST and SECOND SERIES, fcp. 4s. 6d. each.

Lyra Sacra; Hymns, Ancient and Modern, Odes, and Fragments of Sacred Poetry. Edited by the Rev. B. W. SAVILE, M.A. Fcp. 5s.

Lyra Germanica, translated from the German by Miss C. WINKWORTH. FIRST SERIES, Hymns for the Sundays and Chief Festivals; SECOND SERIES, the Christian Life. Fcp. 5s. each SERIES.

Hymns from Lyra Germanica, 18mo. 1s.

Historical Notes to the 'Lyra Germanica:' containing brief Memoirs of the Authors of the Hymns, and Notices of Remarkable Occasions on which some of them have been used; with Notices of other German Hymn Writers. By THEODORE KÜBLER. Fcp. 7s. 6d.

Lyra Eucharistica; Hymns and Verses on the Holy Communion, Ancient and Modern; with other Poems. Edited by the Rev. ORBY SHIPLEY, M.A. Second Edition. Fcp. 7s. 6d.

Lyra Messianica; Hymns and Verses on the Life of Christ, Ancient and Modern; with other Poems. By the same Editor. Fcp. 7s. 6d.

Lyra Mystica; Hymns and Verses on Sacred Subjects, Ancient and Modern. By the same Editor. Fcp. 7s. 6d.

The Chorale Book for England; a complete Hymn-Book in accordance with the Services and Festivals of the Church of England: the Hymns translated by Miss C. WINKWORTH; the Tunes arranged by Prof. W. S. BENNETT and OTTO GOLDSCHMIDT. Fcp. 4to. 12s. 6d.

Congregational Edition. Fcp. 2s.

The Catholic Doctrine of the Atonement; an Historical Inquiry into its Development in the Church: with an Introduction on the Principle of Theological Developments. By H. N. OXENHAM, M.A. formerly Scholar of Balliol College, Oxford. 8vo. 8s. 6d.

From Sunday to Sunday; an attempt to consider familiarly the Weekday Life and Labours of a Country Clergyman. By R. GEE, M.A. Vicar of Abbott's Langley and Rural Dean. Fcp. 5s.

First Sundays at Church; or, Familiar Conversations on the Morning and Evening Services of the Church of England. By J. E. RIDDLE, M.A. Fcp. 2s. 6d.

The Judgment of Conscience, and other Sermons. By RICHARD WHATELY, D.D. late Archbishop of Dublin. Crown 8vo. 4s. 6d.

Paley's Moral Philosophy, with Annotations. By RICHARD WHATELY, D.D. late Archbishop of Dublin. 8vo. 7s.

Travels, Voyages, &c.

Outline Sketches of the High Alps of Dauphiné. By T. G. BONNEY, M.A. F.G.S. M.A.C. Fellow of St. John's Coll. Camb. With 13 Plates and a Coloured Map. Post 4to. 16s.

Ice Caves of France and Switzerland; a narrative of Subterranean Exploration. By the Rev. G. F. BROWNE, M.A. Fellow and Assistant-Tutor of St. Catherine's Coll. Cambridge, M.A.C. With 11 Woodcuts. Square crown 8vo. 12s. 6d.

Village Life in Switzerland. By SOPHIA D. DELMARD. Post 8vo. 9s. 6d.

How we Spent the Summer; or, a Voyage en Zigzag in Switzerland and Tyrol with some Members of the ALPINE CLUB. From the Sketch-Book of one of the Party. In oblong 4to. with about 300 Illustrations, 10s. 6d.

Map of the Chain of Mont Blanc, from an actual Survey in 1863—1864. By A. ADAMS-REILLY, F.R.G.S. M.A.C. Published under the Authority of the Alpine Club. In Chromolithography on extra stout drawing-paper 28in. × 17in. price 10s. or mounted on canvas in a folding case, 12s. 6d.

The Hunting Grounds of the Old World; FIRST SERIES, Asia. By H. A. L. the Old Shekarry. Third Edition, with 7 Illustrations. 8vo. 18s.

Camp and Cantonment; a Journal of Life in India in 1857—1859, with some Account of the Way thither. By Mrs. LEOPOLD PAGET. To which is added a Short Narrative of the Pursuit of the Rebels in Central India by Major PAGET, R.H.A. Post 8vo. 10s. 6d.

Explorations in South-west Africa, from Walvisch Bay to Lake Ngami and the Victoria Falls. By THOMAS BAINES, F.R.G.S. 8vo. with Maps and Illustrations, 21s.

South American Sketches; or, a Visit to Rio Janeiro, the Organ Mountains, La Plata, and the Paraná. By THOMAS W. HINCHLIFF, M.A. F.R.G.S. Post 8vo. with Illustrations, 12s. 6d.

Vancouver Island and British Columbia; their History, Resources, and Prospects. By MATTHEW MACFIE, F.R.G.S. With Maps and Illustrations. 8vo. 18s.

History of Discovery in our Australasian Colonies, Australia, Tasmania, and New Zealand, from the Earliest Date to the Present Day. By WILLIAM HOWITT. With 3 Maps of the Recent Explorations from Official Sources. 2 vols. 8vo. 28s.

The Capital of the Tycoon; a Narrative of a 3 Years' Residence in Japan. By Sir RUTHERFORD ALCOCK, K.C.B. 2 vols. 8vo. with numerous Illustrations, 42s.

Last Winter in Rome. By C. R. WELD. With Portrait and Engravings on Wood. Post 8vo. 14s.

Autumn Rambles in North Africa. By JOHN ORMSBY, of the Middle Temple. With 16 Illustrations. Post 8vo. 8s. 6d.

The Dolomite Mountains. Excursions through Tyrol, Carinthia, Carniola, and Friuli in 1861, 1862, and 1863. By J. GILBERT and G. C. CHURCHILL, F.R.G.S. With numerous Illustrations. Square crown 8vo. 21s.

A Summer Tour in the Grisons and Italian Valleys of the Bernina. By Mrs. HENRY FRESHFIELD. With 2 Coloured Maps and 4 Views. Post 8vo. 10s. 6d.

Alpine Byways; or, Light Leaves gathered in 1859 and 1860. By the same Authoress. Post 8vo. with Illustrations, 10s. 6d.

A Lady's Tour Round Monte Rosa; including Visits to the Italian Valleys. With Map and Illustrations. Post 8vo. 14s.

Guide to the Pyrenees, for the use of Mountaineers. By CHARLES PACKE. With Maps, &c. and Appendix. Fcp. 6s.

The Alpine Guide. By JOHN BALL, M.R.I.A. late President of the Alpine Club. Post 8vo. with Maps and other Illustrations.

Guide to the Western Alps, including Mont Blanc, Monte Rosa, Zermatt, &c. 7s. 6d.

Guide to the Oberland and all Switzerland, excepting the Neighbourhood of Monte Rosa and the Great St. Bernard; with Lombardy and the adjoining portion of Tyrol. 7s. 6d.

Christopher Columbus; his Life, Voyages, and Discoveries. Revised Edition, with 4 Woodcuts. 18mo. 2s. 6d.

Captain James Cook; his Life, Voyages, and Discoveries. Revised Edition, with numerous Woodcuts. 18mo. 2s. 6d.

Narratives of Shipwrecks of the Royal Navy between 1793 and 1857, compiled from Official Documents in the Admiralty by W. O. S. GILLY; with a Preface by W. S. GILLY, D.D. 3rd Edition, fcp. 5s.

A Week at the Land's End. By J. T. BLIGHT; assisted by E. H. RODD, R. Q. COUCH, and J. RALFS. With Map and 96 Woodcuts. Fcp. 6s. 6d.

Visits to Remarkable Places: Old Halls, Battle-Fields, and Scenes illustrative of Striking Passages in English History and Poetry. By WILLIAM HOWITT. 2 vols. square crown 8vo. with Wood Engravings, 25s.

The Rural Life of England. By the same Author. With Woodcuts by Bewick and Williams. Medium 8vo. 12s. 6d.

Works of Fiction.

Late Laurels: a Tale. By the Author of 'Wheat and Tares.' 2 vols. post 8vo. 15s.

A First Friendship. [Reprinted from *Fraser's Magazine.*] Crown 8vo. 7s. 6d.

Atherstone Priory. By L. N. COMYN. 2 vols. post 8vo. 21s.

Ellice: a Tale. By the same. Post 8vo. 9s. 6d.

Stories and Tales by the Author of 'Amy Herbert,' uniform Edition, each Tale *or* Story complete in a single volume.

AMY HERBERT, 2s. 6d. | KATHARINE ASHTON, 3s. 6d.
GERTRUDE, 2s. 6d.
EARL'S DAUGHTER, 2s. 6d. | MARGARET PERCIVAL, 5s.
EXPERIENCE OF LIFE, 2s. 6d. | LANETON PARSONAGE, 4s. 6d.
CLEVE HALL, 3s. 6d. | URSULA, 4s. 6d.
IVORS, 3s. 6d.

A Glimpse of the World. By the Author of 'Amy Herbert.' Fcp. 7s. 6d.

Essays on Fiction, reprinted chiefly from Reviews, with Additions. By NASSAU W. SENIOR. Post 8vo. 10s. 6d.

Elihu Jan's Story; or, the Private Life of an Eastern Queen. By WILLIAM KNIGHTON, LL.D. Assistant-Commissioner in Oudh. Post 8vo. 7s. 6d.

The Six Sisters of the Valleys: an Historical Romance. By W. BRAMLEY-MOORE, M.A. Incumbent of Gerrard's Cross, Bucks. Third Edition, with 14 Illustrations. Crown 8vo. 5s.

The Gladiators: a Tale of Rome and Judæa. By G. J. WHYTE MELVILLE. Crown 8vo. 5s.

Digby Grand, an Autobiography. By the same Author. 1 vol. 5s.

Kate Coventry, an Autobiography. By the same. 1 vol. 5s.

General Bounce, or the Lady and the Locusts. By the same. 1 vol. 5s.

Holmby House, a Tale of Old Northamptonshire. 1 vol. 5s.

Good for Nothing, or All Down Hill. By the same. 1 vol. 6s.

The Queen's Maries, a Romance of Holyrood. 1 vol. 6s.

The Interpreter, a Tale of the War. By the same. 1 vol. 5s.

Tales from Greek Mythology. By GEORGE W. COX, M.A. late Scholar of Trin. Coll. Oxon. Second Edition. Square 16mo. 3s. 6d.

Tales of the Gods and Heroes. By the same Author. Second Edition. Fcp. 5s.

Tales of Thebes and Argos. By the same Author. Fcp. 4s. 6d.

The Warden: a Novel. By ANTHONY TROLLOPE. Crown 8vo. 3s. 6d.

Barchester Towers: a Sequel to 'The Warden.' By the same Author. Crown 8vo. 5s.

Poetry and the Drama.

Select Works of the British Poets; with Biographical and Critical Prefaces by Dr. AIKIN: with Supplement, of more recent Selections, by LUCY AIKIN. Medium 8vo. 18s.

Goethe's Second Faust. Translated by JOHN ANSTER, LL.D. M.R.I.A. Regius Professor of Civil Law in the University of Dublin. Post 8vo. 15s.

Tasso's Jerusalem Delivered, translated into English Verse by Sir J. KINGSTON JAMES, Kt. M.A. 2 vols. fcp. with Facsimile, 14s.

Poetical Works of John Edmund Reade; with final Revision and Additions. 3 vols. fcp. 18s. or each vol. separately, 6s.

Moore's Poetical Works, Cheapest Editions complete in 1 vol. including the Autobiographical Prefaces and Author's last Notes, which are still copyright. Crown 8vo. ruby type, with Portrait, 7s. 6d. or People's Edition, in larger type, 12s. 6d.

Moore's Poetical Works, as above, Library Edition, medium 8vo. with Portrait and Vignette, 14s. or in 10 vols. fcp. 3s. 6d. each

Tenniel's Edition of Moore's *Lalla Rookh,* with 68 Wood Engravings from Original Drawings and other Illustrations. Fcp. 4to. 21s.

Moore's Lalla Rookh. 32mo. Plate, 1s. 16mo. Vignette, 2s. 6d.

Maclise's Edition of Moore's Irish *Melodies,* with 161 Steel Plates from Original Drawings. Super-royal 8vo. 31s. 6d.

Moore's Irish Melodies, 32mo. Portrait, 1s. 16mo. Vignette, 2s. 6d.

Southey's Poetical Works, with the Author's last Corrections and copyright Additions. Library Edition, in 1 vol. medium 8vo. with Portrait and Vignette, 14s. or in 10 vols. fcp. 3s. 6d. each.

Lays of Ancient Rome; with *Ivry* and the *Armada.* By the Right Hon. LORD MACAULAY. 16mo. 4s. 6d.

Lord Macaulay's Lays of Ancient Rome. With 90 Illustratious on Wood, Original and from the Antique, from Drawings by G. SCHARF. Fcp. 4to. 21s.

Poems. By JEAN INGELOW. Ninth Edition. Fcp. 8vo. 5s.

Poetical Works of Letitia Elizabeth Landon (L.E.L.) 2 vols. 16mo. 10s.

Playtime with the Poets: a Selection of the best English Poetry for the use of Children. By a LADY. Crown 8vo. 5s.

Bowdler's Family Shakspeare, cheaper Genuine Edition, complete in 1 vol. large type, with 36 Woodcut Illustrations, price 14s. or, with the same ILLUSTRATIONS, in 6 pocket vols. 3s. 6d. each.

Arundines Cami, sive Musarum Cantabrigiensium Lusus Canori. Collegit atque edidit H. DRURY, M.A. Editio Sexta, curavit H. J. HODGSON, M.A. Crown 8vo. 7s. 6d.

Rural Sports, &c.

Encyclopædia of Rural Sports; a Complete Account, Historical, Practical, and Descriptive, of Hunting, Shooting, Fishing, Racing, &c. By D. P. BLAINE. With above 600 Woodcuts (20 from Designs by JOHN LEECH). 8vo. 42s.

Notes on Rifle Shooting. By Captain HEATON, Adjutant of the Third Manchester Rifle Volunteer Corps. Fcp. 2s. 6d.

Col. Hawker's Instructions to Young Sportsmen in all that relates to Guns and Shooting. Revised by the Author's SON. Square crown 8vo. with Illustrations, 18s.

The Dead Shot, or Sportsman's Complete Guide; a Treatise on the Use of the Gun, Dog-breaking, Pigeon-shooting, &c. By MARKSMAN. Fcp. 8vo. with Plates, 5s.

The Fly-Fisher's Entomology.
By ALFRED RONALDS. With coloured Representations of the Natural and Artificial Insect. 6th Edition; with 20 coloured Plates. 8vo. 14s.

Hand-book of Angling: Teaching Fly-fishing, Trolling, Bottom-fishing, Salmon-fishing; with the Natural History of River Fish, and the best modes of Catching them. By EPHEMERA. Fcp. Woodcuts, 5s.

The Cricket Field; or, the History and the Science of the Game of Cricket. By JAMES PYCROFT, B.A. Trin. Coll. Oxon. 4th Edition. Fcp. 5s.

The Cricket Tutor; a Treatise exclusively Practical. By the same. 18mo. 1s.

Cricketana. By the same Author. With 7 Portraits of Cricketers. Fcp. 5s.

The Horse: with a Treatise on Draught. By WILLIAM YOUATT. New Edition, revised and enlarged. 8vo. with numerous Woodcuts, 10s. 6d.

The Dog. By the same Author. 8vo. with numerous Woodcuts, 6s.

The Horse's Foot, and how to keep it Sound. By W. MILES, Esq. 9th Edition, with Illustrations. Imp. 8vo. 12s. 6d.

A Plain Treatise on Horse-shoeing. By the same Author. Post 8vo. with Illustrations, 2s. 6d.

Stables and Stable Fittings. By the same. Imp. 8vo. with 13 Plates, 15s.

Remarks on Horses' Teeth, addressed to Purchasers. By the same. Post 8vo. 1s. 6d.

On Drill and Manœuvres of Cavalry, combined with Horse Artillery. By Major-Gen. MICHAEL W. SMITH, C.B. Commanding the Poonah Division of the Bombay Army. 8vo. 12s. 6d.

The Dog in Health and Disease. By STONEHENGE. With 70 Wood Engravings. Square crown 8vo. 15s.

The Greyhound in 1864. By the same Author. With 24 Portraits of Greyhounds. Square crown 8vo. 21s.

The Ox, his Diseases and their Treatment; with an Essay on Parturition in the Cow. By J. R. DOBSON, M.R.C.V.S. Crown 8vo. with Illustrations, 7s. 6d.

Commerce, Navigation, and Mercantile Affairs.

The Law of Nations Considered as Independent Political Communities. By TRAVERS TWISS, D.C.L. Regius Professor of Civil Law in the University of Oxford. 2 vols. 8vo. 30s. or separately, PART I. *Peace,* 12s. PART II. *War,* 18s.

A Nautical Dictionary, defining the Technical Language relative to the Building and Equipment of Sailing Vessels and Steamers, &c. By ARTHUR YOUNG. Second Edition; with Plates and 150 Woodcuts. 8vo. 18s.

A Dictionary, Practical, Theoretical, and Historical, of Commerce and Commercial Navigation. By J. R. M'CULLOCH. 8vo. with Maps and Plans, 50s.

The Study of Steam and the Marine Engine, for Young Sea Officers. By S. M. SAXBY, R.N. Post 8vo. with 87 Diagrams, 5s. 6d.

A Manual for Naval Cadets. By J. M'NEIL BOYD, late Captain R.N. Third Edition; with 240 Woodcuts, and 11 coloured Plates. Post 8vo. 12s. 6d.

Works of Utility and General Information.

Modern Cookery for Private Families, reduced to a System of Easy Practice in a Series of carefully-tested Receipts. By ELIZA ACTON. Newly revised and enlarged; with 8 Plates, Figures, and 150 Woodcuts. Fcp. 7s. 6d.

The Handbook of Dining; or, Corpulency and Leanness scientifically considered. By BRILLAT-SAVARIN, Author of 'Physiologie du Goût.' Translated by L. F. SIMPSON. Revised Edition, with Additions. Fcp. 8s. 6d.

NEW WORKS PUBLISHED BY LONGMANS AND CO.   19

On Food and its Digestion; an Introduction to Dietetics. By W. BRINTON, M.D. Physician to St. Thomas's Hospital, &c. With 48 Woodcuts. Post 8vo. 12s.

Wine, the Vine, and the Cellar. By THOMAS G. SHAW. Second Edition, revised and enlarged, with Frontispiece and 31 Illustrations on Wood. 8vo. 16s.

A Practical Treatise on Brewing; with Formulæ for Public Brewers, and Instructions for Private Families. By W. BLACK. 8vo. 10s. 6d.

Short Whist. By MAJOR A. The Sixteenth Edition, revised, with an Essay on the Theory of the Modern Scientific Game by PROF. P. Fcp. 3s. 6d.

Whist, What to Lead. By CAM. Second Edition. 32mo. 1s.

Hints on Etiquette and the Usages of Society; with a Glance at Bad Habits. Revised, with Additions, by a LADY of RANK. Fcp. 2s. 6d.

The Cabinet Lawyer; a Popular Digest of the Laws of England, Civil and Criminal. 20th Edition, extended by the Author; including the Acts of the Sessions 1863 and 1864. Fcp. 10s. 6d.

The Philosophy of Health; or, an Exposition of the Physiological and Sanitary Conditions conducive to Human Longevity and Happiness. By SOUTHWOOD SMITH, M.D. Eleventh Edition, revised and enlarged; with 113 Woodcuts. 8vo. 15s.

Hints to Mothers on the Management of their Health during the Period of Pregnancy and in the Lying-in Room. By T. BULL, M.D. Fcp. 5s.

The Maternal Management of Children in Health and Disease. By the same Author. Fcp. 5s.

Notes on Hospitals. By FLORENCE NIGHTINGALE. Third Edition, enlarged; with 13 Plans. Post 4to. 18s.

C. M. Willich's Popular Tables for Ascertaining the Value of Lifehold, Leasehold, and Church Property, Renewal Fines, &c.; the Public Funds; Annual Average Price and Interest on Consols from 1731 to 1861; Chemical, Geographical, Astronomical, Trigonometrical Tables, &c. Post 8vo. 10s.

Thomson's Tables of Interest, at Three, Four, Four and a Half, and Five per Cent., from One Pound to Ten Thousand and from 1 to 365 Days. 12mo. 3s. 6d.

Maunder's Treasury of Knowledge and Library of Reference: comprising an English Dictionary and Grammar, Universal Gazetteer, Classical Dictionary, Chronology, Law Dictionary, Synopsis of the Peerage, useful Tables, &c. Fcp. 10s.

General and School Atlases.

An Atlas of History and Geography, representing the Political State of the World at successive Epochs from the commencement of the Christian Era to the Present Time, in a Series of 16 coloured Maps. By J. S. BREWER, M.A. Third Edition, revised, &c. by E. C. BREWER, LL.D. Royal 8vo. 15s.

Bishop Butler's Atlas of Modern Geography, in a Series of 33 full-coloured Maps, accompanied by a complete Alphabetical Index. New Edition, corrected and enlarged. Royal 8vo. 10s. 6d.

Bishop Butler's Atlas of Ancient Geography, in a Series of 24 full-coloured Maps, accompanied by a complete Accentuated Index. New Edition, corrected and enlarged. Royal 8vo. 12s.

School Atlas of Physical, Political, and Commercial Geography, in 17 full-coloured Maps, accompanied by descriptive Letterpress. By E. HUGHES F.R.A.S. Royal 8vo. 10s. 6d.

Middle-Class Atlas of General Geography, in a Series of 29 full-coloured Maps, containing the most recent Territorial Changes and Discoveries. By WALTER M'LEOD, F.R.G.S. 4to. 5s.

Physical Atlas of Great Britain and Ireland; comprising 30 full-coloured Maps, with illustrative Letterpress, forming a concise Synopsis of British Physical Geography. By WALTER M'LEOD, F.R.G.S. Fcp. 4to. 7s. 6d.

Periodical Publications.

The Edinburgh Review, or Critical Journal, published Quarterly in January, April, July, and October. 8vo. price 6s. each No.

The Geological Magazine, or Monthly Journal of Geology, edited by HENRY WOODWARD, F.G.S.; assisted by Prof. J. MORRIS, F.G.S. and R. ETHERIDGE, F.R S.E. F.G.S. 8vo. price 1s. each No.

Fraser's Magazine for Town and Country, published on the 1st of each Month. 8vo. price 2s. 6d. each No.

The Alpine Journal: a Record of Mountain Adventure and Scientific Observation. By Members of the Alpine Club. Edited by H. B. GEORGE, M.A. Published Quarterly, May 31, Aug. 31, Nov. 30, Feb. 28. 8vo. price 1s. 6d. each No.

Knowledge for the Young.

The Stepping Stone to Knowledge: Containing upwards of Seven Hundred Questions and Answers on Miscellaneous Subjects, adapted to the capacity of Infant Minds. By a MOTHER. New Edition, enlarged and improved. 18mo. price 1s.

The Stepping Stone to Geography: Containing several Hundred Questions and Answers on Geographical Subjects. 18mo. 1s.

The Stepping Stone to English History: Containing several Hundred Questions and Answers on the History of England. 1s.

The Stepping Stone to Bible Knowledge: Containing several Hundred Questions and Answers on the Old and New Testaments. 18mo. 1s.

The Stepping Stone to Biography: Containing several Hundred Questions and Answers on the Lives of Eminent Men and Women. 18mo. 1s.

Second Series of the Stepping Stone to Knowledge: containing upwards of Eight Hundred Questions and Answers on Miscellaneous Subjects not contained in the FIRST SERIES. 18mo. 1s.

The Stepping Stone to French Pronunciation and Conversation: Containing several Hundred Questions and Answers. By Mr. P. SADLER. 18mo. 1s.

The Stepping Stone to English Grammar: containing several Hundred Questions and Answers on English Grammar. By Mr. P. SADLER. 18mo. 1s.

The Stepping Stone to Natural History: VERTEBRATE OR BACKBONED ANIMALS. PART I. *Mammalia*; PART II. *Birds, Reptiles, Fishes.* 18mo. 1s. each Part.

The Instructor; or, Progressive Lessons in General Knowledge. Originally published under the Direction of the Committee of General Literature and Education of the Society for Promoting Christian Knowledge. 7 vols. 18mo. freely illustrated with Woodcuts and Maps, price 14s.

I. **Exercises, Tales, and Conversations** on Familiar Subjects; with Easy Lessons from History. Revised and improved Edition. Price 2s.

II. **Lessons on Dwelling-Houses** and the Materials used in Building Them; on Articles of Furniture; and on Food and Clothing. Revised and improved Edition. Price 2s.

III. **Lessons on the Universe;** on the Three Kingdoms of Nature, Animal, Vegetable, and Mineral; on the Structure, Senses, and Habits of Man; and on the Preservation of Health. Revised and improved Edition. 2s.

IV. **Lessons on the Calendar and Almanack;** on the Twelve Months of the Year; and on the appearances of Nature in the Four Seasons, Spring, Summer, Autumn, and Winter. Revised and improved Edition. Price 2s.

V. **Descriptive Geography with Popular Statistics** of the various Countries and Divisions of the Globe, their People and Productions. Revised and improved Edition. With 6 Maps. 2s.

VI. **Elements of Ancient History,** from the Formation of the First Great Monarchies to the Fall of the Roman Empire. Revised and improved Edition. Price 2s.

VII. **Elements of [Mediæval and] Modern History,** from A.D. 406 to A.D. 1862: with brief Notices of European Colonies. Revised and improved Edition. Price 2s.

INDEX.

ABBOTT on Sight and Touch	6
ACTON's Modern Cookery	18
AIKIN's Select British Poets	17
——— Memoirs and Remains	3
ALCOCK's Residence in Japan	15
ALLIES on Formation of Christianity	13
Alpine Guide (The)	15
——— Journal (The)	20
APJOHN's Manual of the Metalloids	8
ARAGO's Biographies of Scientific Men	4
——— Popular Astronomy	7
——— Meteorological Essays	7
ARNOLD's Manual of English Literature	5
ARNOTT's Elements of Physics	8
Arundines Cami	17
Atherstone Priory	16
ATKINSON's Papinian	4
Autumn Holidays of a Country Parson	6
AYRE's Treasury of Bible Knowledge	13
BABBAGE's Life of a Philosopher	3
BACON's Essays, by WHATELY	4
——— Life and Letters, by SPEDDING	3
——— Works, by ELLIS, SPEDDING, and HEATH	4
BAIN on the Emotions and Will	6
——— on the Senses and Intellect	6
——— on the Study of Character	6
BAINES's Explorations in S.W. Africa	15
BALL's Guide to the Central Alps	15
——— Guide to the Western Alps	15
BAYLDON's Rents and Tillages	12
BLACK's Treatise on Brewing	19
BLACKLEY and FRIEDLANDER's German and English Dictionary	5
BLAINE's Rural Sports	17
BLIGHT's Week at the Land's End	16
BONNEY's Alps of Dauphiné	15
BOURNE's Catechism of the Steam Engine	12
——— Handbook of Steam Engine	12
——— Treatise on the Steam Engine	11
BOWDLER's Family SHAKSPEARE	17
BOYD's Manual for Naval Cadets	18
BRAMLEY-MOORE's Six Sisters of the Valleys	16
BRANDE's Dictionary of Science, Literature, and Art	9
BRAY's (C.) Education of the Feelings	7
——— Philosophy of Necessity	7
——— (Mrs.) British Empire	7
BREWER's Atlas of History and Geography	19
BRINTON on Food and Digestion	19
BRISTOW's Glossary of Mineralogy	8
BRODIE's (Sir C. B.) Psychological Inquiries	7
——— ——— Works	10
——— ——— Autobiography	10
BROWNE's Ice Caves of France and Switzerland	15
BROWNE's Exposition 39 Articles	12
——— Pentateuch	12
BUCKLE's History of Civilization	2
BULL's Hints to Mothers	19
——— Maternal Management of Children	19
BUNSEN's Analecta Ante-Nicæna	13
——— Ancient Egypt	2
——— Hippolytus and his Age	13
——— Philosophy of Universal History	13
BUNSEN on Apocrypha	13
BUNYAN's Pilgrim's Progress, illustrated by BENNETT	11
BURKE's Vicissitudes of Families	4
BURTON's Christian Church	3
BUTLER's Atlas of Ancient Geography	19
——— Modern Geography	19
Cabinet Lawyer	19
CALVERT's Wife's Manual	14
Campaigner at Home	6
CATS and FARLIE's Moral Emblems	11
Chorale Book for England	14
COLENSO (Bishop) on Pentateuch and Book of Joshua	13
COLUMBUS's Voyages	16
Commonplace Philosopher in Town and Country	6
CONINGTON's Handbook of Chemical Analysis	9
CONTANSEAU's Pocket French and English Dictionary	5
——— Practical ditto	5
CONYBEARE and HOWSON's Life and Epistles of St. Paul	12
COOK's Voyages	16
COPLAND's Dictionary of Practical Medicine	10
——— Abridgment of ditto	10
Cox's Tales of the Great Persian War	2
——— Tales from Greek Mythology	16
——— Tales of the Gods and Heroes	16
——— Tales of Thebes and Argos	16
CRESY's Encyclopædia of Civil Engineering	11
Critical Essays of a Country Parson	6
CROWE's History of France	2
D'AUBIGNÉ's History of the Reformation in the time of CALVIN	2
Dead Shot (The), by MARKSMAN	17
DE LA RIVE's Treatise on Electricity	8
DELMARD's Village Life in Switzerland	15
DE LA PRYME's Life of Christ	13
DE TOCQUEVILLE's Democracy in America	2
Diaries of a Lady of Quality	3
DOBSON on the Ox	18
DOVE's Law of Storms	7
DOYLE's Chronicle of England	2

Edinburgh Review (The)	20
Ellice, a Tale	16
ELLICOTT's Broad and Narrow Way	13
———— Commentary on Ephesians	13
———— Destiny of the Creature	13
———— Lectures on Life of Christ	13
———— Commentary on Galatians	13
———————— Pastoral Epist.	13
———————————— Philippians,&c.	13
———————————————— Thessalonians	13
Essays and Reviews	13
——— on Religion and Literature, edited by MANNING	13
——— written in the Intervals of Business	6
FAIRBAIRN's Application of Cast and Wrought Iron to Building	11
——————— Information for Engineers	11
——————— Treatise on Mills & Millwork	11
FFOULKES's Christendom's Divisions	13
First Friendship	16
FITZ ROY's Weather Book	7
FOWLER's Collieries and Colliers	12
Fraser's Magazine	20
FRESHFIELD's Alpine Byways	15
——————— Tour in the Grisons	15
Friends in Council	6
FROUDE's History of England	1
GARRATT's Marvels and Mysteries of Instinct	8
GEE's Sunday to Sunday	14
Geological Magazine	8, 20
GILBERT and CHURCHILL's Dolomite Mountains	15
GILLY's Shipwrecks of the Navy	16
GOETHE's Second Faust, by Anster	17
GOODEVE's Elements of Mechanism	11
GORLE's Questions on BROWNE's Exposition of the 39 Articles	12
Graver Thoughts of a Country Parson	6
GRAY's Anatomy	10
GREENE's Corals and Sea Jellies	8
——————— Sponges and Animalculae	8
GROVE on Correlation of Physical Forces	8
GWILT's Encyclopædia of Architecture	11
Handbook of Angling, by EPHEMERA	18
HARE on Election of Representatives	5
HARTWIG's Sea and its Living Wonders	8
——————— Tropical World	8
HAWKER's Instructions to Young Sportsmen	17
HEATON's Notes on Rifle Shooting	17
HELPS's Spanish Conquest in America	2
HERSCHEL's Essays from the Edinburgh and Quarterly Reviews	9
——————— Outlines of Astronomy	7
HEWITT on the Diseases of Women	9
HINCHLIFF's South American Sketches	15
Hints on Etiquette	19
HODGSON's Time and Space	7
HOLLAND's Chapters on Mental Physiology	6
——————— Essays on Scientific Subjects	9
——————— Medical Notes and Reflections	10
HOLMES's System of Surgery	10
HOOKER and WALKER-ARNOTT's British Flora	9
HORNE's Introduction to the Scriptures	13

HORNE's Compendium of the Scriptures	13
HOSKYNS's Talpa	12
How we Spent the Summer	15
HOWITT's Australian Discovery	15
——————— History of the Supernatural	6
——————— Rural Life of England	16
——————— Visits to Remarkable Places	16
HOWSON's Hulsean Lectures on St. Paul	12
HUGHES's (E.) Atlas of Physical, Political, and Commercial Geography	19
——————— (W.) Geography of British History	7
——————— Manual of Geography	7
HULLAH's History of Modern Music	3
——————— Transition Musical Lectures	3
HUMPHREYS' Sentiments of Shakspeare	11
Hunting Grounds of the Old World	13
Hymns from *Lyra Germanica*	14
INGELOW's Poems	17
Instructor (The)	20
JAMESON's Legends of the Saints and Martyrs	11
——————— Legends of the Madonna	11
——————— Legends of the Monastic Orders	11
JAMESON and EASTLAKE's History of Our Lord	11
JOHNS's Home Walks and Holiday Rambles	8
JOHNSON's Patentee's Manual	11
——————— Practical Draughtsman	11
JOHNSTON's Gazetteer, or Geographical Dictionary	7
JONES's Christianity and Common Sense	7
KALISCH's Commentary on the Old Testament	5
——————— Hebrew Grammar	5
KENNEDY's Hymnologia Christiana	14
KESTEVEN's Domestic Medicine	10
KIRBY and SPENCE's Entomology	9
KNIGHTON's Story of Elihu Jan	16
KÜBLER's Notes to Lyra Germanica	14
KUENEN on Pentateuch and Joshua	13
Lady's Tour round Monte Rosa	15
LANDON's (L. E. L.) Poetical Works	17
Late Laurels	16
LATHAM's English Dictionary	5
LECKY's History of Rationalism	2
Leisure Hours in Town	6
LEWES's Biographical History of Philosophy	2
LEWIS on the Astronomy of the Ancients	4
——— on the Credibility of Early Roman History	4
——————— Dialogue on Government	4
——— on Egyptological Method	4
——————— Essays on Administrations	4
——————— Fables of BABRIUS	4
——— on Foreign Jurisdiction	4
——— on Irish Disturbances	4
——— on Observation and Reasoning in Politics	4
——— on Political Terms	4
——— on the Romance Languages	4
LIDDELL and SCOTT's Greek-English Lexicon	5
——————— Abridged ditto	5
LINDLEY and MOORE's Treasury of Botany	9

LONGMAN's Lectures on the History of England	1
LOUDON's Encyclopædia of Agriculture	12
———— Cottage, Farm, and Villa Architecture	12
———— Gardening	12
———— Plants	9
———— Trees and Shrubs	9
LOWNDES's Engineer's Handbook	11
Lyra Domestica	14
—— Eucharistica	14
—— Germanica	11, 14
—— Messianica	14
—— Mystica	14
—— Sacra	14
MACAULAY's (Lord) Essays	2
————History of England	1
————Lays of Ancient Rome	17
————Miscellaneous Writings	6
————Speeches	5
————Speeches on Parliamentary Reform	5
MACDOUGALL's Theory of War	12
MARSHMAN's Life of Havelock	3
McLEOD's Middle-Class Atlas of General Geography	19
———— Physical Atlas of Great Britain and Ireland	19
McCULLOCH's Dictionary of Commerce	18
———— Geographical Dictionary	7
MACFIE's Vancouver Island	15
MAGUIRE's Life of Father Mathew	3
———— Rome and its Rulers	3
MALING's Indoor Gardener	9
MASSEY's History of England	1
MASSINGBERD's History of the Reformation	3
MAUNDER's Biographical Treasury	4
———— Geographical Treasury	7
———— Historical Treasury	2
———— Scientific and Literary Treasury	9
———— Treasury of Knowledge	19
———— Treasury of Natural History	9
MAURY's Physical Geography	7
MAY's Constitutional History of England	1
MELVILLE's Digby Grand	16
———— General Bounce	16
———— Gladiators	16
———— Good for Nothing	16
———— Holmby House	16
———— Interpreter	16
———— Kate Coventry	16
———— Queen's Maries	16
MENDELSSOHN's Letters	3
MENZIES' Windsor Great Park	12
—— on Sewage	12
MERIVALE's (H.) Colonisation and Colonies	7
———— Historical Studies	1
———— (C.) Fall of the Roman Republic	2
———— Romans under the Empire	2
———— on Conversion of Roman Empire	2
—— on Horse's Foot	18
—— on Horse Shoeing	18
—— on Horses' Teeth	18
—— on Stables	18
MILL on Liberty	4
——on Representative Government	4
——on Utilitarianism	4
MILL's Dissertations and Discussions	4
————Political Economy	4
————System of Logic	4
————Hamilton's Philosophy	4
MILLER's Elements of Chemistry	9
MONSELL's Spiritual Songs	14
———— Beatitudes	14
MONTAGU's Experiments in Church and State	13
MONTGOMERY on the Signs and Symptoms of Pregnancy	9
MOORE's Irish Melodies	17
————Lalla Rookh	17
————Memoirs, Journal, and Correspondence	3
————Poetical Works	17
MORELL's Elements of Psychology	6
———— Mental Philosophy	6
Morning Clouds	14
MORTON's Prince Consort's Farms	12
MOSHEIM's Ecclesiastical History	13
MÜLLER's (Max) Lectures on the Science of Language	5
———— (K. O.) Literature of Ancient Greece	2
MURCHISON on Continued Fevers	10
MURE's Language and Literature of Greece	2
New Testament illustrated with Wood Engravings from the Old Masters	10
NEWMAN's History of his Religious Opinions	3
NIGHTINGALE's Notes on Hospitals	19
ODLING's Course of Practical Chemistry	9
————Manual of Chemistry	9
ORMSBY's Rambles in Algeria and Tunis	15
OWEN's Comparative Anatomy and Physiology of Vertebrate Animals	8
OXENHAM on Atonement	14
PACKE's Guide to the Pyrenees	15
PAGET's Lectures on Surgical Pathology	10
———— Camp and Cantonment	15
PEREIRA's Elements of Materia Medica	10
———— Manual of Materia Medica	10
PERKINS's Tuscan Sculpture	11
PHILLIPS's Guide to Geology	8
————Introduction to Mineralogy	8
PIESSE's Art of Perfumery	12
———— Chemical, Natural, and Physical Magic	12
———— Laboratory of Chemical Wonders	12
Playtime with the Poets	17
Practical Mechanic's Journal	11
PRESCOTT's Scripture Difficulties	13
PROCTOR's Saturn	7
PYCROFT's Course of English Reading	5
———— Cricket Field	18
———— Cricket Tutor	18
———— Cricketana	18
READE's Poetical Works	17
Recreations of a Country Parson, SECOND SERIES	6
REILLY's Map of Mont Blanc	15
RIDDLE's Diamond Latin-English Dictionary	5
———— First Sundays at Church	14
RIVERS's Rose Amateur's Guide	9

24   NEW WORKS PUBLISHED BY LONGMANS AND CO.

ROGERS's Correspondence of Greyson...... 6
———— Eclipse of Faith.................. 6
———— Defence of ditto 6
———— Essays from the *Edinburgh Review* 6
———— Fulleriana 6
ROGET's Thesaurus of English Words and Phrases 5
RONALDS's Fly-Fisher's Entomology 18
ROWTON's Debater...................... 5
RUSSELL on Government and Constitution . 1

SAXBY's Study of Steam 19
———— Weather System................. 7
SCOTT's Handbook of Volumetrical Analysis 9
SCROPE on Volcanos 8
SENIOR's Biographical Sketches 4
———— Historical and Philosophical Essays........................ 2
———— Essays on Fiction............... 16
SEWELL's Amy Herbert................... 16
———— Ancient History................. 2
———— Cleve Hall 16
———— Earl's Daughter................. 16
———— Experience of Life 16
———— Gertrude...................... 16
———— Glimpse of the World........... 16
———— History of the Early Church..... 3
———— Ivors 16
———— Katharine Ashton............... 16
———— Laneton Parsonage 16
———— Margaret Percival 16
———— Night Lessons from Scripture.... 14
———— Passing Thoughts on Religion.... 14
———— Preparation for Communion..... 14
———— Readings for Confirmation 14
———— Readings for Lent............. 14
———— Self-Examination before Confirmation................... 14
———— Stories and Tales 16
———— Thoughts for the Holy Week..... 14
———— Ursula 16
SHAW's Work on Wine 19
SHEDDEN's Elements of Logic 5
Short Whist 19
SHORT's Church History 3
SIEVEKING's (AMELIA) Life, by WINKWORTH 3
SIMPSON's Handbook of Dining........... 18
SMITH's (SOUTHWOOD) Philosophy of Health 19
———— (J.) Voyage and Shipwreck of St. Paul 13
———— (G.) Wesleyan Methodism 3
———— (SYDNEY) Memoir and Letters.... 4
———————— Miscellaneous Works .. 6
———————— Sketches of Moral Philosophy 6
———————— Wit and Wisdom 6
SMITH on Cavalry Drill and Manœuvres.... 18
SOUTHEY's (Doctor) 5
———— Poetical Works................ 17
SPOHR's Autobiography 3
Spring and Autumn 14
STANLEY's History of British Birds........ 8
STEBBING's Analysis of MILL's Logic...... 5
STEPHENSON's (R.) Life by JEAFFRESON and POLE 3
STEPHEN's Essays in Ecclesiastical Biography........................... 4

STEPHEN's Lectures on the History of France 2
Stepping Stone to Knowledge, &c........... 20
STIRLING's Secret of Hegel.............. 6
STONEHENGE on the Dog................ 18
———— on the Greyhound 18

TASSO's Jerusalem, by JAMES............ 17
TAYLOR's (Jeremy) Works, edited by EDEN 14
TENNENT's Ceylon 8
———— Natural History of Ceylon 8
THIRLWALL's History of Greece 2
THOMSON's (Archbishop) Laws of Thought 4
———— (J.) Tables of Interest 19
———— Conspectus, by BIRKETT...... 10
TODD's Cyclopædia of Anatomy and Physiology 10
———— and BOWMAN's Anatomy and Physiology of Man 10
TROLLOPE's Barchester Towers 16
———— Warden 16
TWISS's Law of Nations 18
TYNDALL's Lectures on Heat............. 8

URE's Dictionary of Arts, Manufactures, and Mines 11

VAN DER HOEVEN's Handbook of Zoology 3
VAUGHAN's (R.) Revolutions in English History 1
———— (R. A.) Hours with the Mystics 7
VILLARI's Savonarola 3

WATSON's Principles and Practice of Physic 10
WATTS's Dictionary of Chemistry.......... 9
WEBB's Celestial Objects for Common Telescopes 7
WEBSTER & WILKINSON's Greek Testament 13
WELD's Last Winter in Rome............. 15
WELLINGTON's Life, by BRIALMONT and GLEIG 3
———— by GLEIG 3
WEST on the Diseases of Infancy and Childhood 9
WHATELY's English Synonymes 4
———— Logic 4
———— Remains..................... 4
———— Rhetoric 4
———— Sermons.................... 14
———— Paley's Moral Phylosophy.... 14
WHEWELL's History of the Inductive Sciences........................... 2
Whist, what to lead, by CAM 19
WHITE and RIDDLE's Latin-English Dictionary............................ 6
WILBERFORCE (W.) Recollections of, by HARFORD 3
WILLIAMS's Superstitions of Witchcraft .. 6
WILLICH's Popular Tables 19
WILSON's Bryologia Britannica........... 9
WOOD's Homes without Hands 8
WOODWARD's Historical and Chronological Encyclopædia 2

YONGE's English-Greek Lexicon 5
———— Abridged ditto 5
YOUNG's Nautical Dictionary............. 18
YOUATT on the Dog 18
———— on the Horse 13

SPOTTISWOODE AND CO., PRINTERS, NEW-STREET SQUARE, LONDON

www.ingramcontent.com/pod-product-compliance
Lightning Source LLC
Chambersburg PA
CBHW020123170426
43199CB00009B/609